PRAISE FOR SUSAN M. TIBERGHIEN
AND *FOOTSTEPS: IN LOVE WITH A FRENCHMAN*

"*Footsteps: In Love with a Frenchman* is a charming, heartfelt journey
into European culture and cuisine, the beauty and loneliness of
unfamiliar places, and the exquisite good fortune of finding a
lifelong companion. Tiberghien's essays are a rich bouillabaisse
of scenic detail and delicious memories. Just a lovely book."

— Dinty W. Moore, author of *Dear Mister Essay Writer Guy:
Advice and Confessions on Writing, Love, and Cannibals*

"Susan Tiberghien's memoir is a love story and from that
matrix a meditation about many kinds of love. Light and
dark days, funny and momentous ones, are celebrated and
define this family's cross-cultural journey. The pages fly by and
before we know it, the six children have grown into adults. In
the new silence, familiar footsteps insist that she write."

— Wallis Wilde-Menozzi, author of *Mother
Tongue: An American Life in Italy*

"Stitched together from essays, poems, photographs and even family
recipes, Susan Tiberghien's elegant memoir combines all the intimacy
of a family album with the wisdom of her vivid prose and poetry."

— Elaine Vitone, contributor to *Creative Nonfiction*

"Susan Tiberghien's poetic memoir evokes a life fully lived and
closely observed. In elegant prose and poetry, she presents the
landscapes of her time with fresh eyes, gentle humor, and a
generous spirit. This is a wise book and a pleasure to read."

—Peter Meinke, author of *Lucky Bones*

D0775316

FOOTSTEPS

IN LOVE WITH A FRENCHMAN

ALSO BY SUSAN M. TIBERGHIEN

Side by Side: Writing Your Love Story
One Year to a Writing Life: Twelve Lessons to Deepen Every
Writer's Art and Craft
Looking for Gold: A Year in Jungian Analysis
Circling the Center: One Woman's Encounter with Silent Prayer

Susan M. Tiberghien

FOOTSTEPS

IN LOVE WITH A FRENCHMAN

 Red Lotus Studio Press

Red Lotus Studio Press
New York, New York
Facebook.com/RedLotusStudioPress
info@theredlotusreview.com

Publisher: Melissa A. Rosati
Copy Editor: Betsy Robinson
Cover, text design and typography by Infinitum Limited.
Printed by CreateSpace, a DBA of On-Demand Publishing, LLC
This book is available for wholesale and retail distribution
through Amazon Extended Distribution.

First Red Lotus Studio Press edition 2015, expanded and revised
First published in 2004 as *Footsteps: A European Album, 1955 – 1990*

Red Lotus Studio Press books are available at special
discounts for bulk purchases in the United States by
corporations, institutions, and other organizations. For more
information, please contact info@theredlotusreview.com

Published in the United States by Red Lotus Studio
Press, a DBA of Melissa's Coaching Studio, LLC.

ISBN 978-0-9961660-0-3 (paper)—ISBN 978-0-9961660-2-7 (ebook)

Photography credits are listed at the end of the text.

Contents

Introduction

FOOTSTEPS: IN LOVE WITH A FRENCHMAN RELATES THE stories of a journey, a journey that each of us is called to make as we set out to find our way home.

From the start, *Footsteps* created itself. I am an American-born writer, residing in Switzerland. After raising a large family in Europe, I returned to writing full-time and published narrative essays about everyday life in different cultures. Seeing the appeal of these stories, I gathered many of them together into a collection, along with some prose poems and photographs of the beautiful places where I have lived.

The subject I know well. I have lived it—tasted it, listened to it, smelled it. My experience of crossing cultures has been from the inside. Married to a Frenchman, the oldest son in a patriarchal family of ten children, I followed him to France, Belgium, Italy, and Switzerland, raising six children in French, Italian, and English.

The audience of the essays I know well. First published in *The Christian Science Monitor, The London Financial Times,*

The International Herald Tribune, the Messenger, they were then republished in anthologies, more recently *Swaying* (U. of Iowa), *Tanzania on Tuesday* (New Rivers Press), *Ticking Along Free* (Bergli Books, Switzerland), *The Circle Continues* (Innisfree Press).

And I know how helpful these essays are as tools for teaching. Each year, since 1990, I have used them in workshops at writers' conferences in Geneva, Paris, New York; for the International Women's Writing Guild in New York, Boston, Chicago, Orlando, Santa Fe; and at C. G. Jung Centers across the States. I have discovered how these stories speak to readers, encouraging them to deepen their creativity and share their own stories.

In our contemporary world of multi-cultured settings, we long for a deeper sense of belonging. In *Footsteps: In Love with a Frenchman*, the reader discovers not only other countries and other cultures, but more importantly the reader discovers the underlying kinship that unites us.

As we search for meaning in our lives, we are seeking a single—and universal—homeland.

This book is dedicated to the Frenchman with whom I have been in love for almost sixty years, and to our children and grandchildren. Each of the stories is but a small thank you for the immense happiness they have given me.

I wish to thank also all my writing friends on both sides of the ocean who first encouraged me to put these stories together into a collection. And especially my amazing editor and publisher, Melissa Rosati, at Red Lotus Studio Press who encouraged me to enlarge the collection with additional stories and lots more intrigue, laughter, and love.

FRANCE
1955 – 1960

Grenoble in the 1950s

Swaying

WHEN I WAVED GOODBYE ON DECK OF THE *LIBERTÉ*, MY parents said "Don't fall in love with a Frenchman!" I laughed and said, "Of course not."

I arrived in the fall, fresh out of college, with years of French behind me, only to discover that I couldn't pronounce the name of the place where I was going. Grenoble. Or rather I couldn't pronounce it the French way. When I'd try to tell people where I was going—in Le Havre where the boat docked or in Paris where I stopped en route—they would look at me and say "*Pardon?*" They made it sound like another place. I said Grenoble, they said *Pardon*.

They didn't know what I was talking about, and I didn't know what they were talking about. I kept thinking it would be a matter of weeks and I would become fluent, but it was more a matter of months. Day after day, I'd smile and listen, then smile and listen again. And day after day I'd understand a few more words, and then a few more.

Grenoble in the 1950s was a handsome city in the heart of the French Alps. Wrought-iron balconies decorated the facades of gray stone buildings, and dark red roofs slanted toward the sky. Wide boulevards crossed the city, each one ending in snow-covered mountains. The university buildings were in *la Vieille Ville* close to the winding river, with its old stone bridges and the cable car going up to the *Bastille* on the side of one of the mountains.

I went to the registration office and learned that there were no student dormitories for women, only for men. I was on my own, with a city map and a list of private rooms for rent. I started with addresses close to the university buildings. First I would ask to see the room. Then I'd ask to see the bathroom. The landlady would shake her head, no bathroom, only a sink in a corner of the room and a water closet in the hall or halfway down the staircase.

I was beginning to lose hope when finally one lofty lady showed me a large tiled bathroom with a grand white bathtub standing on giant lion paws. I didn't think to ask whether there was hot water. I settled into a bare room and, after bracing myself through a couple of cold baths, inquired after hot water. My landlady said there wasn't any but there were public baths—with hot water—on the other side of the city. So once a week, with my cake of soap and a large bath towel, I'd take the trolley and stand in line inside the bathhouse, waiting for my tubful of steaming hot water. Sometimes I'd fill it twice and happily soak until someone knocked on the door.

In the dead of winter, the water froze in the pipes along the outside wall of the apartment building. We had no running water, and still worse, we had no heat. My landlady took to wearing her fur coat, fur hat, and fur boots during the day, but I didn't have any furs. I wrapped myself in woolen blankets and woolen socks, scarves and mittens. Finally I started studying in a café close by and stayed in my room only to sleep, all dressed up and wearing my boots.

I was supposed to be studying contemporary French literature. I therefore registered at the *Faculté des Lettres* and chose courses that were related to the twentieth century. They were all lecture courses given in large halls, destined to house hundreds of French students. *Hélas*, I was unable to understand more than one sentence at a time so I dropped my morning lectures to go to French classes. In the afternoon I returned to the *Faculté*, choosing this time courses taught by the professors who spoke the slowest. It didn't matter what the subject was. Weeks later when I found myself taking notes directly in French, I realized something had happened. My mind had switched to French.

However, that was only half of becoming fluent. I was understanding but I was not being understood. I could see people wince when I mispronounced a word. After many long weeks of practice, I learned the French *R*. I could almost say "Gre-noble" and gargle the *R* out correctly. But there was still something amiss.

A professor said it was my nasal consonantal diphthongs. He said they exploded in my mouth. French was a romantic language. Only when I could correctly pronounce *un bon vin blanc*, would I be truly fluent. I repeated the sounds, "*un, on, in, an*," trying to hold my breath at the same time. Finally the diphthongs became softer, more subtle, and with many evenings of wine tasting, I was able to ask for a good white wine and be understood each time.

Next came ski lessons. Everyone in Grenoble skied, and each Saturday the university ski club organized lessons on the mountains close by. We went on busses, scooting and skidding up steep, narrow icy roads. Upon my arrival, the instructors asked me if I had skied before. "*Oui*," I nodded, and they put me on the cable car right up to the top of Chamrousse, where the Olympic giant slalom run was held the following year. No one asked me when or where I had skied. If I had told them it was ten years ago on a snow-covered golf course in the suburbs of New York City, they wouldn't have believed me.

So up I went to the top of the mountain. When we began putting on our skis, I couldn't figure out where to put my feet or how to work the clamps. The instructor thought I was joking. Then we started down the mountain, about ten of us, one behind the other. It was snowing, and our instructor kept shouting back, *aval* or *amont*. One means to turn on the upper ski, the other means to turn on the lower ski. It was snowing so hard that it really didn't matter, I couldn't see the difference. At the bottom of the trail, the instructor counted to make certain we were all there.

The next week when I went back in sunny weather and saw the slope, or rather the side of the mountain I had skied down, I tried to say there had been a mistake. I said I was only a beginner. Wasn't there another slope, a less steep slope, a lower-down slope? But it was too late; I was already in the same cable car on my way back up.

I took my meals at a student hall where the dining room was on the second floor, which for the French is the first floor. Instead of lining up downstairs, everyone would plow their way into the wide stone staircase. At first I thought I'd be able to help them understand how much simpler it would be if they waited their turn in line. But this was out of the question; anything resembling a line was simply not French. This particular line in wintertime, with all the snow and ice on our boots, was treacherous. More than once, several of us slid backward, only to be pushed forward by those behind us, as if we were changing gears. No one ever really fell. There wasn't room. In fact it became sort of fun. Each evening before dinner, we would sway back and forth together.

Inside the dining room, I always sat at the same table and listened to the same group of students. They'd discuss everything with the same passion, be it ski or Marx, pasta or Mendelssohn. There were two girls in the group and five boys. The girls mostly listened, although they had no evident problem with their diphthongs. The boys never listened; they talked all at once. Some were Catholic, others were Communist, some were both, others were neither.

There was a war going on in the French colony of Algeria. Some students were for the French staying in, others were for the French getting out. During the same evening that some would be picketing a talk on *Algérie française*, the others would be inside listening. I tried both: one evening listening inside, the next evening picketing outside. Afterwards we'd all go out together.

There was little pairing off and dating. When I explained how in the States we first dated, then went steady, then got pinned, and only then did we get engaged, they were dumbfounded. They shook their heads and said it sounded all too much like standing in line. So wherever we went, we would pile onto scooters, the girls with their arms around whomever was in front of them.

In the evening, we would go for coffee at *la Place Grenette* in the heart of the *Vieille Ville*. We'd order eight *café-filtres*. On top of each cup sat a little metal filter, with very black, freshly ground coffee at the bottom and hot water on top. We'd wait for the water to seep through, sometimes trying to hurry it along, most of the time forgetting it. The coffee was lukewarm at its best, but very dark. We'd stay late into the night, discussing our favorite jazz musicians, the books we were reading, the war in Algeria. The boys would order cognac. The girls would dip sugar cubes into the glasses. Each cube was called a *canard*, a duck.

ॐ

In May, over a long weekend, one of the group organized a student trip to Venice. He asked me to go along just for the company. I looked forward to seeing Venice and the different visits along the way, both going and coming back. But when I overslept the morning we were to leave, he had the tour bus come right underneath my window in the center of the city and the chauffeur honk the horn. The others waited patiently while I gathered my things all carefully prepared the night before, hurried out the door of the apartment, and ran down the dark staircase to the street. From then on, Pierre kept me up front with him so I wouldn't get lost.

On our way back we stopped to spend a day and a night at Bellagio, a small picturesque fishing village jutting out into the middle of Lago di Como. In the early afternoon, a few of us took a motorboat across the blue-green lake to the Villa Carlotta and its famed seventeenth century garden landscaped with terraces, stairs, statues, fountains—where the monumental azaleas and rhododendrons, riotous with color and perfume, hugged the wide slopes reaching down to the water.

We walked down the narrow shaded lanes. Somehow in the maze of all the flowers, Pierre and I found ourselves alone. The bushes, their branches laden with blossoms, were taller than we. They opened their arms, then closed them behind us. The luscious flowers—scarlet, bright pink, fuchsia—glowed in the sunlight. Their sweet fragrance made me light-headed. Pierre bent down and lifted up my face.

And unexpectedly I fell in love with a Frenchman. I stopped worrying about my consonantal diphthongs, they started to come naturally. And when I went back to the States in the summer, I no longer wanted to stand in line. Instead I wanted to sway.

Cloister, Pavia   *Gardens, Lago di Como*

Snow-covered Trail, Haute Savoie

Footsteps

IT WAS IN THE DEAD OF WINTER DURING MY FIRST YEAR in France. The snowflakes swirled in all directions as the dull yellow headlights wedged forward. We were three inside the car: Alain who was driving, Pierre whose younger sister had died a few hours earlier, and me.

The 2CV climbed the snow-piled roads leading into the mountains north of Grenoble. I pulled up my coat collar and blew on my cold fingertips.

"Here, take my scarf," said Pierre from the backseat, handing me his red woolen scarf.

"No, you keep it.

"Go ahead, put it around you."

The snow thickened. I could see nothing ahead or to the sides, only shades of snow, shutting out the world around us.

"What a night to die," Pierre said. "Ever since she came home from nursing school, I guess we should have known. Lung cancer at twenty-one. The doctors said it goes fast at that age. But three months?"

Alain didn't answer. He was leaning forward, his forehead almost touching the windshield. Every now and then there was a gust of wind, lifting the curtain of snow, and we could see a meter or two in front of us. There were no other cars.

"All the family will be there," Pierre continued. "When Papa telephoned, he didn't say much. Only that she died quietly."

I listened. His younger sister was my age, twenty-one. I drew his woolen scarf up around my neck and dug my cold hands into the pockets of my coat.

"During the Christmas holidays," he kept on, "she appeared to be getting better. My younger brothers started spending most of their time in her room." Pierre couldn't stop talking. "She'd read to them and tell them stories. They seemed to understand better than the rest of us. They weren't afraid."

Not afraid? When I was seven, my grandmother died. She had been sick and bedridden and was living with us. I never saw her dead. My parents thought I was too young. I looked out the window into the blinding snow.

Suddenly the car lurched sideways, the two front wheels spun on ice, and we bucked over the side of the road. There was a dreadful thud as the car gave one last jolt, a race horse missing the final hurdle.

"Christ, that's it. I'm off the road," said Alain, turning off the engine. "All for one small patch of ice."

"I was talking too much," said Pierre. "We're not far from la Roche. We'll walk, and I'll call my father to come fetch us."

The three of us got out. Our boots sunk into the snow. In the middle of the street was a streak of ice, where an invisible stream had tried to cross and then froze in its path. The falling snow lightened the blackness of the night. I braced my shoulders and back against the cold.

"How're you doing?" asked Pierre, sheltering me on one side. Alain stayed close on the other side. We walked along silently. The road started to climb. The cold made it difficult to breathe.

"We'll soon be there," said Pierre.

I wondered where "there" was. I wondered where we were. It was only a few months earlier that I had arrived in Grenoble.

We kept on walking. Soon a few houses appeared on either side of the road. All the shutters were closed. Finally, the village square of La Roche, where a light glimmered behind the windowed door of a café. We went inside. Pierre telephoned his father.

"He'll come get us. You'll both sleep at the house."

"No, not the night of your sister's death," said Alain, "We'll look for a hotel."

"Not at midnight. My parents are expecting you."

I didn't know what to say. Until skidding off the road, I was expecting to be back in my bed in Grenoble by midnight.

Outside the wind screeched against the shutters. We waited and listened. At last, the lights of a car were reflected in the frosted pane of the door.

Pierre's father entered with a blast of freezing wind. He took his oldest son in his arms, then stepped toward Alain and me.

"I'm sorry about this," he said. "We'll take care of the car tomorrow. First, we'll find you warm beds at the house."

We went outside into the storm. The snow swirled in gusts. I climbed into the big car and huddled into a corner of the backseat. The men talked in spurts. Everything was foreign—the country, the language, the storm.

"We're here," said Pierre's father. In front of us was a large house with lights shining in all the windows. Pierre's mother opened the front door. Young children crowded around her.

We climbed the few front steps. Pierre's mother embraced him and then greeted Alain and me. Her eyes were swollen but she offered us a smile. One of Pierre's brothers took our coats.

"Perhaps you first want to go upstairs and see Christine," said his mother.

Pierre and Alain moved toward the staircase.

I started to shiver. See Christine? A dead person? There in the house? I stood still, rubbing my cold hands together.

His mother looked at me. "You must be exhausted. I'll show you to your room and you can get some rest."

We walked up the flight of stairs. Pierre and Alain continued up another flight to Christine's bedroom. His father and younger brothers followed. I watched them disappear as his mother led me to a small room half under the staircase. It was all white—the walls, the table, and piles of linen.

"I'm sorry to give you the linen room, but it's the only room left." She pulled down a folding bed from a closet in the wall. It too had white covers.

I wanted to thank her, to excuse myself, to say something about Christine, but I could not find the words.

"It's all right," she said. "Try to get some rest. I hope you'll be comfortable." She closed the door behind her.

I sat down on the narrow bed. Opposite me on the floor, a row of black shoes lined the white wall. Pierre had seven younger brothers. Their shoes were waiting to be polished for the funeral. Soon there would also be Pierre's. Eight pairs of black shoes in a line.

Outside the dormer window, the snow was still falling heavily. I listened as more footsteps went up and down the stairs. I turned off the one overhead light and crawled under the cold covers. The piles of white linen surrounded me like the high snowbanks along the road. And against the wall, the black shoes glowed in the dark.

The house was awake, keeping watch over Christine. I lay very still on my back. The steps marshaled the silence. I started to count them. Pierre and Alain, were they still, upstairs? And the younger brothers, the ones who listened to her stories, were they also upstairs?

Christine who was my age, where was she now? Life, death. Why was I so afraid? My grandmother was different. She was old. Christine was too young. Why? Where was God?

I closed my eyes. I saw again the snowstorm. I felt the car skidding. We were again walking along the snow-piled mountain road. It was dark. Then I was walking alone. The swirling snowflakes lit my way. I kept walking. I had to get to the top.

I opened my eyes. The footsteps above my head continued to echo in the stairwell. They climbed, they descended. Pierre,

Alain, the younger brothers, the mother, the father. Whose steps were whose? I listened to the heavy ones, to the light ones. I imagined my own.

The storm quieted. My heart quieted.

In the morning, I watched the sky lighten—immense and blue. The whole world glistened with fresh snow. There was a tap on my door. It was Pierre. The family was waiting for me downstairs at the breakfast table.

Steps

THERE IS A GAME I PLAYED AS A CHILD. THE LEADER would say, "Take one giant step." And I'd stretch my leg clear across the ocean. "Take two baby steps." I'd make my baby steps as big as possible. "Now a giant step back." I'd pretend to stretch way back. "A giant step forward." I'd spring ahead.

There is a dream I kept alive. I am building a bridge across the ocean. The bridge curves and rises gently up and down. There are sidewalk cafés and inns with window boxes of red geraniums. Terraces reach out over the swelling waves. I am walking to Europe.

There are steps swaying back and forth. I sway with them. Old steps, new steps. Steps walking in the snow. I see them in the dark. Steps going up and down. I hear them echo in the stairwell. Steps of children, each one different. I let them go.

Countryside, Provence

Spécialité Provençale

IT WAS SUMMERTIME WHEN WE ARRIVED IN THE SMALL village of Istres with its white walls and red sunbaked roofs, built on a hillside in southern France. Pierre was assigned to the Air Force base camouflaged in the fields of lavender surrounding the village.

I was an American bride, learning to be a French housewife. In the fifties in Provence, there were no supermarkets, no Colgate toothpaste, no Coca-Cola, no paper bags. Each day I bought a *baguette* of bread at the bakery, cheese at the dairy shop, meat at the butcher's, vegetables and fruit at the open-air market. And each day I carried it all home in my straw basket.

Nor were there refrigerators. I kept the milk in an earthenware pitcher wrapped with a damp dishtowel outside on the windowsill. The mistral, the strong northerly wind, cooled it even on the hottest of summer days. Nor were there washing machines. I washed everything in the bathtub, including the sheets and the towels. They dried in no time on the line outside the window, near the milk pitcher.

ॐ

During my apprenticeship, I learned to count on my next-door neighbor, Madame Michel, an imposing woman, surely twice my age and twice my size, steel-gray hair in tight ringlets, corpulent and corseted.

Shortly after my arrival I went and rang her doorbell. Coming from the other side of the ocean, I wanted to introduce myself. Slowly she took me under her wide wing.

"*Pauvre petite dame*," she'd say, "here all alone, with a husband away day and night at the air base."

My spoken French made her scowl. For more than a year she tried to teach me to roll my *R*s. It already was difficult to make them guttural. Now my next-door neighbor wanted me to make them *provençale* at the same time. I tried but knew I'd never succeed.

ॐ

When Madame Michel learned that I was expecting my first baby that winter, she told me about her first baby—how huge he was and how she thought she was going to die right on the kitchen table in her house. She said after that she made sure there'd never be another.

She told me I should eat garlic, raw garlic, every day. "You'll see, it will keep your muscles soft and ease the delivery," she said.

I nodded and hoped my muscles would stay soft without the garlic diet.

She suggested we go garlic picking every Friday morning. It grew wild in large clumps near the fields of lavender. We pulled it up by the armful. On the way home, she'd tear a bunch apart and squeeze out the cloves for me to chew.

At first I tried to say I that I would wait for lunch, and then I just stuck the cloves in my mouth and chewed along.

ॐ

She found my husband very handsome in his Air Force uniform, with the gold-buttoned jacket and gold-trimmed hat, and invited us to Sunday dinner, requesting that Monsieur come fully dressed. Pierre told me that meant in his full dress uniform. Madame Michel wasn't a churchgoer but said she'd hold dinner for us until after Sunday Mass.

When we rang her doorbell, she was dressed in black as usual, but for the occasion she was wearing a polished yellow stone which glowed fiercely on her bosom. In the dining room there lingered a musty odor mixed with lavender. Three places were set on the starched white cloth.

"I've made a surprise for you," she called from the kitchen, *"paella provençale."*

She carried in a large round earthenware dish. The yellow saffron rice was ringed with onions, tomatoes, olives, and mushrooms, and in the middle rested a rabbit's head, its eyes staring straight at me.

"There're the best part of the paella," said Madame Michel. "There's one for each of you.

Pierre and I declined. I quickly looked away, but not soon enough. She had picked up the rabbit's head and was sucking out each round, beady eye.

ॐ

It was a very cold winter. Our landlord told us it was an exception. Madame Michel went to call on him, insisting that he install something to heat the apartment and keep us from freezing.

"Imagine, the baby coming and no heat!" she said. In her house she had radiators but never used them. She said it wasn't worth the fuss since she lived alone.

So our landlord came and put a wood stove in our kitchen. When Pierre was home, he tended it. When he was working at the air base, Madame Michel tended it. Certain that her American neighbor knew nothing about French wood stoves, she'd watch for when I was alone and then come tapping at our door.

Soon she'd be poking around in the pot-bellied stove, shoving the wood back and forth, and sure enough the fire would glow for the rest of the day.

One Sunday morning I woke up to a snowstorm. Pierre was away at the air base. Madame Michel was hammering at the kitchen door.

"I thought you'd freeze and never wake up," she said, carrying in an armful of wood

When I told her I was late for church, she said it didn't matter. People didn't go to church when it snowed. "Besides," she chided, "you're getting too pregnant to go to church. In your condition, you shouldn't show yourself so much."

I told her I still was going. She shook her head and said something I didn't understand. I bundled warmly and trudged up the narrow street to the old stone church built when the village was more prosperous and its people more churchgoing. With the light snow falling, everything was still and pristine.

The church was nearly empty, and I huddled up front with a few other churchgoers. The priest arrived late, his black cassock and black beret dusted with flakes of snow. He told us we had gained in the grace of the Lord and could now go back home. There would be no Mass.

Shortly after the snowstorm, I started having labor pains and Pierre drove me to the hospital. The birth was very long and laborious in spite of Madame Michel's garlic. Pierre fell fast asleep while reading Marcel Pagnol aloud. I was no longer listening.

When finally the nurse wheeled me into the delivery room, the doctor had gone home long ago. Only the midwife, short and squat, was still waiting. As the pains shot through me, I thought about Madame Michel on her kitchen table.

The midwife told me to push harder. She pushed with me until at last it was over, and the baby was there. It was a boy. We named him Pierre, after his father and grandfather. And William as a middle name, after my father and grandfather

Madame Michel came to visit. She appeared awed, almost afraid. She said it was the first time she'd ever set foot inside a hospital. Staring at the baby swaddled in white in the small crib, she quickly brushed away tears.

"Maybe I should have had another baby," she said. "But not on the kitchen table."

I never learned where her one child lived. He had moved away long ago; that was all Madame Michel told me. And she never told me anything about her husband. Each time she got near, she'd fall silent.

She lived alone in her house with dust covers on the furniture. She must once have had several people at her large table. The sounds and smells were still there in the shadows, along with the china, crystal, and silver.

"I don't have company anymore," she told me. "There's no one around."

When I'd ask her to come and have supper with us, she always refused, saying that she was better off keeping to herself. And every night at nine o'clock sharp I'd see her light go out.

In the springtime, my husband watched her hoe and plant a vegetable garden on her side of the fence. Madame Michel told him he could come and help her. She said he could turn over the earth in the corner and plant whatever he wanted. He asked if she knew anything about planting corn.

"Corn," she repeated, looking at him as if he'd lost his mind. "What are you thinking of doing with corn?"

Pierre said he was thinking of eating it. He explained that he had tasted it the first time fresh from his father-in-law's garden in the States. It was sweet and tasted a little like fresh green peas.

"Well," she said, shaking her heavy shoulders in disbelief, "you just try eating the corn that grows around here. It sure isn't sweet peas."

We wrote to ask my father how he planted his corn. An envelope of pink-colored grains arrived with a long sheet of handwritten instructions. Pierre made ready a patch of earth and planted half of the package.

Madame Michel stood watch as ten cornstalks raised their heads out of the ground. Soon one cob of corn appeared on each stalk. Madame Michel would pull back the husks, just a little at a time, when she thought I wasn't looking, and take a good long sniff at the kernels.

Once the corn was ripe, she finally accepted an invitation to Sunday dinner at noon. I picked six of the cobs and served them steaming hot. Madame Michel didn't say much, she was too busy chewing every kernel off her cob, and then off the extra three.

ₔ

Before we were to leave the village, Madame Michel wanted to make us another Provençal dish. "No rabbit this time," she promised. "Only fish. I'll make you a real bouillabaisse,

bouillabaisse provençale. Invite some of your friends and I'll come make it for you."

This way, she added, I wouldn't need to move the baby and carry him next door. She told me that babies should stay put, especially in the evenings. She scolded me plenty and hugged me tight.

"Then you'll stay and eat with us," I answered.

"No, not in the evening."

The day of the bouillabaisse, she arrived early in the morning with bundles of fish, bought at the market and wrapped in newspaper. She undid them at the sink and started splashing away, slitting open bellies, slashing off heads and tails. Blood, scales, and other bits splattered around the sink and over the wall. I disappeared into the bedroom to nurse the baby, closing the door behind me.

Madame Michel was still at the sink when I came back. She held up each cleaned fish and rattled off the names: *"raie, rouget, rascasse..."* I wondered if she had purposely chosen fish whose names began with *R*. She set them aside to be cooked at the last minute, put everything else into my biggest pot, and told me to let it simmer all day.

When she went home at noon, I washed down the wall and opened wide the windows.

She came back in late afternoon to make the *rouille*, a garlic and red pepper sauce, grinding it with a pestle into a fine paste in an old wooden bowl which she'd brought with her. I opened the window still wider. From time to time she'd taste a bit on her finger. Then she'd taste a spoonful of soup. And then she'd dip in one of the croutons she was making and taste one, and then another.

When finally the seasoning was right, the soup was strained, the fish was cooked, and the croutons were golden, I asked her once again to stay. She shook her head and said she'd eaten enough.

৵

It was soon time to pack our belongings and leave La Provence. Pierre had finished his military service. We were moving to Brussels where he was going to work for the Common Market. I was going to have supermarkets once again—Colgate toothpaste, Coca-Cola, and paper bags—and central heating and people speaking English.

I never liked leaving a place, wanting instead to take it with me. And so I wanted to take along Madame Michel, the wood stove, the corn patch, the paella, without the rabbit's head.

We found the little package of pink corn grains which my father had sent us from the States and tried to give what was left to Madame Michel.

"*Mon Dieu, non,*" she said. "I wouldn't know what to do with it."

Our small car—a gray 2CV—was packed. We still didn't have any furniture, just ourselves and our first baby, along with the straw basket for shopping and a few odds and ends for keeping house that I had found in the village.

Madame Michel came to say goodbye. She looked at us and sighed heavily. "Now be off with you."

She hugged little Pierre, or Peter as I was calling him. She let big Pierre kiss her on each cheek. And then she clasped me close in her strong arms.

"*Adieu, ma petite dame.* I'll miss you. I never had a real neighbor before."

MADAME MICHEL'S BOUILLABAISSE
(for four)

—◄o►—

Place in casserole 2 pounds assorted fish

skatefish (raie)	*flounder (limande)*
red mullet (rouget)	*burbot (baudroie, lotte)*
scorpion fish (rascasse)	*John Dory (saint-pierre)*
cray fish (écrevisse)	

Sauté 2 onions in 2 T. olive oil, pour over fish. Add 2 T. tomato paste, 3 branches fennel, 4 bay leaves, 2 branches rosemary, 2 t. saffron, 6 cloves of garlic, salt, pepper, ¼ cup olive oil. Marinate a few hours, stirring now and then.

For the next step, place 8-10 peeled new potatoes on top. Cover with *soupe de poisson* and cook for 20 minutes.

To serve, place potatoes on one platter, fish on another, and soup, with small toasts rubbed with garlic, in a bowl. Accompany with a small bowl of *rouille*.

SOUPE DE POISSON

Sauté 1 onion in 1 T. olive oil, add 1 pound fish (bits&pieces). Simmer for 20 minutes. Add 1 T. tomato paste, 3 branches fennel, 3 bay leaves, 1 t. saffron, 4 cloves garlic, salt, pepper. Cover with water (6 to 8 cups). Boil for 20 minutes, strain.

ROUILLE

Soak 2 small dried peppers for 10 minutes, peel them, add 3 crushed cloves of garlic, 1 potato, 1 T. olive oil, ½ cup soup.

BELGIUM
1961 – 1964

La Grande Place, Bruxelles

Lace Curtains

IT TOOK US THREE TRIES TO FIND A HOME IN BRUSSELS. Our first try was an apartment in the middle of a row of red brick houses—each with spotless front windows and lace curtains.

The house reminded Pierre of his parents' house in northern France but then they had the whole three floors. We had just the top floor. His parents also had a parlor maid who slept under the roof and who kept the front windows sparkling. I didn't want a parlor maid or a three-floor, red brick row house. I wanted a one-story wooden ranch house, in a large, open yard with forsythia bushes and birch trees.

Ours was a furnished apartment including everything from a legion of laundry lines that descended from the ceiling in the bathroom to a special feather duster "to be used only for picture frames and lamp shades," the landlady informed me. There was a twelve-page inventory listing even the number of hangers in each closet, "to be signed by Monsieur," she said.

Our apartment went from the front bedroom to the back kitchen, with the living room in the middle without any windows. We lived most of the time in the kitchen where there was a big bay window. One-year-old Peter sat on the floor and played with the different items on the inventory. His favorite was an old-fashioned coffee grinder that had a tiny drawer to collect the ground coffee.

Whenever I wanted to go out, I had to carry Peter down the two steep staircases, get him into the baby carriage stored under the stairs, then hold open the front door while bouncing the carriage and Peter down the five front steps. When number two was on her way, we decided it was time to leave the row house and look for something closer to the ground, something with a little yard and lots of windows.

Our second try was half of a brand new house in the outskirts of Brussels, built on a little plot of ground with a patch of grass for Peter to play outside. It still wasn't a ranch house but it was all ours. This time it was not furnished, no lace curtains, no old-fashioned coffee grinder, no twelve-page inventory. Instead, two floors of empty space. We bought a double bed. Friends lent us a kitchen table, some chairs, and a sofa. Our voices resounded through the empty hallways and rooms.

Our second baby was a girl, born a year and a half after her brother. Pierre's mother again lent us the white baby crib that had served for her ten children. We gave it another layer of paint and put it in the smallest of the empty bedrooms.

We bought a child-sized bed for Peter and put it in the second empty bedroom.

The rest of the house we furnished slowly. First we had to make up our minds whether we wanted my choice of style which was Danish modern on wall-to-wall carpeting, or Pierre's choice which varied between the eighteenth and nineteenth century on oriental rugs. When Pierre's grandparents—living nearby in northern France—gave us a large Persian carpet, I relented on the wall-to-wall carpeting. Then when his aunts and uncles—also living nearby in northern France—gave us an antique walnut secretary, I also relented on the Danish modern.

Often on Saturday we'd go to the outdoor flea market— *le marché aux puces*—to shop for antique tables, armchairs, picture frames. Soon I found myself looking forward to our weekend treasure hunts. We got to know some of the *marchands*. They would always have a *bonbonnière* filled with caramels for the children. And sometimes a glass of wine for the parents.

The first months in our new home were quiet summer days. But after their vacations—as the Belgians returned from the seacoast—our quiet corner was transformed into a noisy intersection. Cars swished past us on either side nonstop. Pierre said the only place where he didn't hear the din of traffic was in the bathtub with his head under the water.

Then one morning, bliss. We overslept. There was no noise. We turned over in bed and listened. Nothing. It was unreal. We looked out the window and, behold, it was snowing.

Over twenty centimeters of fresh snow lay on the ground, and not one car was in sight.

ès

After the snow melted, we made a third try at house hunting. I was no longer looking for a ranch house. We were looking for something quiet. We went to the ground floor of an old-fashioned stone and stucco apartment building, situated on a small side street which no one knew about and where there was no traffic.

There was a maid's room on the top floor which we used as an attic. Outside, in the back, we had a little courtyard all to ourselves, with a cherry tree, a pebbled circular path, and a gentle slope in the back corner. Peter played there riding his tricycle and pulling his new red wagon. Soon his little sister joined him.

Our front hall was large and long, running the length of the apartment. I liked the polished oak floors and bought an electric waxer. There were gas burners to heat the water and a coal furnace to heat the radiators. Early each morning Pierre would fetch a bucket of coal from the bin in the cellar.

We were back in the center of the city. I made white lace curtains for the front windows and then for the back windows. Soon I was happily expecting our third child. We brought down the white baby crib from the attic. Then we decided to bring down everything and make the attic room back into a maid's room. We were going to have our first *fille au pair*. She wouldn't be a parlor maid to keep the front windows clean, but rather a mother's helper and we'd clean the windows together.

And so the old-fashioned apartment fit us well. It had taken three tries in three years to find us a home. I was no longer dreaming about an American ranch house or Danish furniture. Our apartment had lace curtains and smelled of antique furniture wax. I was even beginning to grind fresh coffee beans every day, with my own wooden coffee grinder that I found at the flea market.

Birthdays

WE WERE EXPECTING OUR THIRD CHILD FOR PIERRE'S thirtieth birthday. He told me not to worry about celebrating until after the baby was born. "*Une chose à la fois,*" he said. One thing at a time. "First you have the baby, and then I'll have my birthday."

So we spent the day quietly at home. It was Ascension Thursday, a national church holiday in Belgium and the beginning of a long four-day weekend, a good time to have a baby. Pierre wouldn't have to go to work until Monday. He'd be home to take care of the children and to come see me and the new baby at the hospital.

The morning passed and nothing happened. Instead of feeling sluggish, I felt full of energy and high spirits. I straightened the house, played with the children, and every now and then I gazed at the baby's crib—the same one we had used for the first two, the white lining again washed and ironed. I was looking forward to the luxury of almost a week's rest, of people taking care of me. My suitcase was ready and filled with journals and books.

As the afternoon got underway, we decided to go for a walk. I thought the fresh air and exercise would be good for all of us and hoped that it would be especially good for me and make the baby come. Waiting made Pierre nervous. As soon as I would look a bit tired, or would stop to catch my breath, he'd ask, "Are you all right?" "Are you in pain?" "Can I do something?" "Should I call the doctor?"

The May weather was sunny and delightful. We went for a walk around one of the ponds at Wolluwe, where there are rolling green lawns and circular shaded paths. We watched the ducks skim along the top of the water. I wondered when I would be able to skim along, slim and lithesome.

I stopped waddling along and started to run, just a little, behind the children. Pierre told me to stop. He did not think it was good for me to run around. "Besides, you really are very pregnant," he said. "People are looking at you. Very pregnant women don't go running around ponds in Brussels."

It was only when we arrived back home that I told him I didn't feel well. He said I shouldn't have run around the pond. I reminded him that we both wanted the baby to come that day, on his birthday, and that it was a good day for going to the hospital. He said even so I should try to be a little more sedate, maybe a little more Belgian.

He took care of feeding the children while I lay down to rest in our bedroom. Occasionally I sort of sighed and shuddered. Pierre kept coming to ask if I was all right, if he could do something, if he should call someone. I told him everything was normal, the contractions were starting, and I started to sigh and shudder quite regularly.

He finally said he was going for the babysitter, as we had arranged in case the labor should start. She lived on the outskirts of the city. Then he would take me to the hospital. He didn't want to wait any longer.

"But it's just the beginning," I said. "It's probably still too early."

"Yes, but who knows. It's a third baby. Maybe this one will come more quickly than the others. You know, you should not have run this afternoon." He was apprehensive and wanted to get the babysitter to the apartment right away. "Is there still time?" he asked.

"Yes, there's time."

He hesitated. "Are you sure?"

"Yes, I am sure."

He told the children to be good and to play quietly in their room and not to disturb their mother in any way. He would be back as soon as possible and then he would take their mother to the hospital. He told them that their little brother or sister would soon be there.

It was exactly seven o'clock. The timing was perfect. As soon as he left, I got up and told the children we were going to celebrate their father's birthday. They looked at me in wide disbelief. Four-year-old Peter said he thought I was going to have a baby.

"I will, dear," I said, "but not just yet. First we're going to surprise your father."

The doorbell rang and the first guests arrived. They brought with them a huge birthday cake, iced in white, with thirty red, white, and blue candles, "for France and America!" Our children rose to the occasion. More friends—Belgian, Dutch, French, German, Italian—kept coming. They were all intrigued with my proposed American way of celebrating birthdays.

Everyone was to arrive at 7:10 sharp, with their cars parked on another street, unless of course I telephoned to cancel. It would take Pierre a little over a half hour to fetch the sitter. There was just time to welcome everyone and help them hide out of sight.

Our bedroom, the intended dining room of the apartment, opened into the living room through two French doors. When they were opened, there were hiding places for everyone. This would be a surprise party like the ones I used to enjoy in the States. I only hoped that Pierre would also enjoy it.

Some of the guests hid behind the drapes, some went behind the couch and the armchairs. As people got into the swing of it, two or three climbed into the wardrobe closet. Others disappeared under the dining table, and a few last Belgians, who had been reluctant at first, gamely crawled under our bed. I lay down on my side of the bed and let the two children hide under the covers on their father's side.

We were ready.

We waited. It seemed like hours when it was only minutes. There were over twenty of us hiding together in the two rooms.

No one dared speak or hardly breathe. There wasn't a sound. The air became electric. The children were stunned into silence.

I heard his key at the front door.

"Susie?" he called.

"I'm here." I couldn't say one more word for fear I'd give it all away. I lay back in the bed and listened.

Pierre said something to the babysitter and walked down the hall to the bedroom door. I waited, holding my breath. I heard each footstep. He gently turned the knob and opened the door.

"*Bonne anniversaire!*"

"Happy Birthday!"

"Surprise!"

Friends raised their heads from behind the couch, climbed out of the cupboard, disentangled themselves from the curtains, pulled themselves out from under the bed. Our children scrambled out from under the covers. I stood up and went to the door.

Pierre shook his head in dismay. Then he managed a grin and gave me a hug as close as he could.

We had the long weekend to rest. Sunday we went for another walk back around the pond of Wolluwe. The ducks were still skimming over the top of the water. This time I didn't run behind the children. I didn't feel up to it. Number three was on her way. She was born that evening, thirty years and three days after her father.

CANAPÉS

—◄o►—

Let's think of canapés for twenty guests. Imagine small
slices from a long baguette. People might each eat four of
them. So here are four ideas. Make twenty of each!

BLUE CHEESE WITH ARMAGNAC
Soften 6 T. blue cheese with 2 T., butter and mix in an ounce of Armagnac
(Cognac will do). Spread on slices of bread, lightly toasted, and top each
canapé with a hazelnut.

SHRIMP ON CUCUMBER
Place a small shrimp on a slice of cucumber. First spread a thin layer of
mayonnaise on the toast, then the cucumber and the shrimp. Decorate with
a caper.

ASPARAGUS AND PARMA HAM
Wrap two or three lightly salted asparagus tips in a small slice of Parma ham.
Place on toasted bread slices with a thin layer of mayonnaise.

SMOKED SALMON AND CRÈME FRAÎCHE
Try using small blinis. Spread lightly with crème fraîche (thick sour cream),
then curl a small narrow slice of smoked salmon on top. Decorate with
fresh dill.

"Remember?"

OUR CHILDREN REMEMBER THE LITTLE SLOPE IN OUR back courtyard as a big hill. They would pull their red wagon up to the top and push off to the grass below. Sometimes they'd take their stuffed animals along, telling them to hold on tight. If they fell out, they'd tell them to hold on still tighter.

This was back in the early 1960s, when we believed in peace and good will around the world. There was J. F. Kennedy and Pope John XXIII. In Brussels, we were living the early days of the European Community. My husband was seeing research projects move ahead. There would be a united Europe. There'd be no more borders, there'd be a common currency. Our children would go to European schools, they would have European passports. They would proclaim themselves Europeans.

On Sundays, we welcomed friends and neighbors to our apartment. Students from my English classes would come and sometimes stay for supper. Two Libyan students showed us how to make their North African couscous, with lots of chili, coriander, and cumin. A Chadian student, Adda—tall, with tribal marks on his handsome cheeks—taught our children to clap their hands as if playing a drum while he moved in rhythm to the beat.

Our children were growing up contentedly. Their father worked close by, I stayed mostly at home, playing with them, letting them draw and paint, taking them to the park with other mothers and children. In the evening we'd read them stories, their father in French and their mother in English. It was a time when everything seemed possible.

So when a young American artist asked for a place to exhibit his paintings, we offered our apartment. It wasn't large but it was central. The day of the exhibit, friends helped us move out furniture, take off doors, clear the walls. We were expecting close to fifty people from all around the world.

The artist hung his larger canvasses in the front hall—flamboyant circus figures in bright blues, greens, and yellows. The largest canvas was of a clown with a lopsided smile, holding on to a big yellow balloon. The artist put it at the end of the hall where it could be seen from everywhere. The smaller canvasses he put in the living room.

The first guests arrived. We introduced them to the artist and to each another. More guests arrived. People liked the bold, brightly colored figures in the paintings. Pierre served glasses of wine and fruit juice. The children passed trays filled with canapés. The circus came to life, full of expectancy and enthusiasm, a carousel on the walls of our apartment.

The phone rang. It was an American friend who worked at the Embassy, saying he wished to excuse himself. He wouldn't be able to come to the exhibit. I asked why.

"I'd like to wait and tell you later," he replied.

"Why?" I asked again. "What's happened?"

"President Kennedy's been shot."

I saw our guests caught up in the dream of bright blues and yellows. I hung up and looked for my husband. Together we went outside. While we were standing on the front steps, the chauffeur of one of our African guests came to find us.

"Is my boss at your place?" he asked.

We nodded.

"Do you know what's happened?"

"You mean President Kennedy?" asked Pierre.

"Yes, sir. I heard it on the car radio. Please, sir, don't tell my boss. He'll burst out crying in front of everyone." He looked at both of us. "Let me tell him when he's safe in the car."

We went back into the apartment. The paintings and the people swirled in a bright merry-go-round. Our children were still up, moving from one room to another. I stayed near the door, waiting for the African diplomat to leave.

Again the phone rang. It was another American calling to excuse himself. The news was confirmed. President Kennedy had been assassinated, in a parade in Dallas. It was time to put our children to bed and tell our guests.

Minutes passed. We stood together, shocked into silence. We looked for something to hold on to, something to steady us. So many of us were far from our home countries. We needed support. Slowly our guests gathered their coats and filed out into the black night.

Our apartment never felt the same. The children still pulled their wagon up the small slope. We still read them stories before bedtime. Students and friends still dropped in. But the exuberance had disappeared. We looked at our children and felt vulnerable.

Years later, after we moved to Italy, the children would sometimes speak about the courtyard with the gentle slope behind our apartment. They remembered playing with their wagon on the hill. "It was a real big hill," they would say. "Remember?"

ITALY
1965 – 1968

Church, Northern Italy

Aggiornamento

EARLY ONE SATURDAY MORNING, SHORTLY AFTER OUR move to northern Italy, there was a knock on our front door. I opened it to Don Francesco, the village priest. Dressed in his long black cassock, he was accompanied by two young altar boys in white robes with lace collars. Our children hid behind me, holding tight to my bathrobe.

"*Signora*, excuse me," Don Francesco stammered, blushing with confusion. "I have come too early. I wanted to bless your new home."

"Please, come in." Fairly new to the Catholic faith, I had never attended a house blessing. I stood back to let him enter. Seeing that he was hesitating, I added, "My husband will be back shortly, he went to buy some rolls at the bakery."

Don Francesco, followed by the two young altar boys, advanced into our apartment. He produced a small glass vase filled with holy water from the folds of his long robe. Reciting something in Latin, he started to sprinkle holy water around our home. The altar boys with their lace collars bowed their heads each time Don Francesco raised his arm.

We watched the little procession move into each room. The breakfast table, unmade beds, dolls and stuffed animals, even the bath towels, everything got blessed.

When Don Francesco finished, I thanked him and offered him a cup of coffee.

"Oh no, *Signora*, thank you."

"Please do come back," I said.

Don Francesco's glasses slipped down the bridge of his nose.

"I mean when my husband is home."

"*Si, Signora*, when your husband is home," he repeated. Then he backed out the front door, followed by the two altar boys.

I learned that it was the yearly custom for the village priest to bless the homes of his parishioners who in turn gave an annual offering. Not a cup of coffee. Don Francesco was to come back each year, and each year the blessing would be updated to comply with the *aggiornamento* of the Church. We were living the last years of the Second Vatican Council, and the Italian clergy was adapting—with a certain gusto—to the new rules.

The second year Don Francesco arrived at our door with only one altar boy who was no longer wearing a white robe or a lace collar. This time my husband was home. I was no longer still in my bathrobe, and our children were not hiding behind me. They stood back respectfully. Don Francesco did not stammer.

His glasses did not slip down his nose. The blessing was limited to the living room and the front hall.

"It's not the number of blessings which counts, but the intention," said Don Francesco.

"Yes, of course," I said.

I liked the rituals of the Church, and it felt good to be part of this common prayer for homes and families.

࿐

The third year Don Francesco came alone. The altar boys were no longer performing any duties outside the walls of the church. Our children greeted him and asked where he was hiding the holy water. They looked in the pockets of his long black cassock and found only caramel candies.

"But look, there is still another pocket," he said, uncovering still another fold and pulling out the same little vase intact with holy water.

The children wanted to see if there were also more caramels. Don Francesco laughed and found still more.

He then proceeded to bless the front entrance. "One blessing is quite sufficient," he said.

And this time the one blessing was in Italian.

I was disappointed. The Latin had been part of the tradition.

࿐

The fourth year, our last year in Italy, Don Francesco came once again alone. He was dressed as a clergyman, in a neatly tailored black suit. There was no room for the vase and the holy

water, only for a few caramels for the children. He assured us
that he could still bless the house.

"The holy water is not really essential," he said.

Even the children looked disappointed.

"But Don Francesco," said my husband, "what did you do
with your old cassocks?"

"Look," he answered, turning around to show off his well-
fitted black suit. "There's a tailor in town who recycles them.
He has a very good business." Don Francesco made a sign of
the cross and stayed for a cup of coffee.

Black and White

EVERYTHING WAS WHITE EXCEPT THE BLACK BEARD OF the Italian doctor. I watched it move back and forth across the white room.

"You know," said the doctor to my husband behind me, "I once lost a woman after it was all over. She had her whole family in here celebrating with champagne. It was a boy." He walked to the side and pulled on white gloves. "I still had some sewing to do. She wanted anesthesia. Then damn if her heart didn't stop."

I gripped the armrests.

"Please, *Signora*, continue. It is not yet over. You must not stop." He moved back to the center. "Now where was I? Yes, with the woman from Rome. There she was dead and all around her people were drinking champagne."

The room split open.

The doctor stopped talking and held up the baby. "*Brava, Signora. Bravissima*! It's a boy."

"Please, Doctor," I said, "no champagne."

Our Balcony, Comerio

Quarantine Regulations

FOR FOUR YEARS WE LIVED IN A BIG WHITE APARTMENT house overlooking the village of Comerio and in the distance Lago Maggiore. The stone lane leading up the hill to the big white house was only wide enough for one car, and even the telephone didn't make it up the hill until we were packing to leave. Our Italian baby doctor never understood how an American mother, with an ever-growing brood of children, could survive without a phone on a one-way hillside.

With each emergency I'd run down the lane to the public pay-phone in the village café to call the doctor. He would obligingly come as soon as possible, driving up the hillside, honking his horn all the way, until he turned safely into the parking place in front of the house.

One winter morning our two girls awoke, both with a dull red rash covering their bodies. Their skin felt like patches of sandpaper. Pierre was leaving for work, taking our oldest son to the school bus on his way.

I got out my Dr. Spock book on childcare and looked at what he had to say about rashes. Reading along, I started to suspect scarlet fever: "...tiny red spots on flushed skin." Dr. Spock went on to specify that "quarantine regulations vary a great deal in different localities." As I ran down the hill to the telephone, I wondered about regulations in Italian localities.

The doctor arrived at noon and examined both girls. He nodded his head. It was scarlet fever.

"I must tell you," he said, "that here in the village children with scarlet fever are taken straight away to the hospital in Varese." He asked if he could wash his hands.

"I probably can get around that," he continued, "but the girls will have to remain in strict quarantine and not venture out of the apartment."

"For how long?" I asked.

"For six weeks." He kept scrubbing his hands.

"And their older brother?" I asked, handing him a clean towel. "What about him?"

"He'll have to stay home from school for three weeks." He carefully dried each hand. "*Si, Signora*, these are the regulations."

"And the baby?"

He stopped for a moment and then remembered. "Since you're nursing him, he should be all right. But he should be kept separate, different room, you know, different towels, different games."

I did know. I also knew enough not to ask about the father and mother, and whether we should be kept separate.

We complied with the regulations. The girls didn't venture outside the door of the apartment for six weeks. Their rash soon disappeared. Their older brother, surprised to be on vacation, happily stayed home from school for three weeks, and their baby brother liked all the company. Even Pierre started coming home from work at lunchtime.

Our Italian neighbors inquired after our health. They would come to the door to ask about the children, but they never crossed the doorstep. As it happened no one else got scarlet fever—no one in our family, no one in the large white house, no one in the entire village.

਍਍

At the end of the six-week siege, two men in white trousers and white jackets appeared one morning at our front door. The girls were playing outside in the terraced yard, relieved and happy to be released from the apartment.

"Sanitary officers from the village," they said, bowing with ceremony. They looked more like astronauts, each with a space gun slung over his shoulder.

"Yes?"

"We've come to disinfect the sick room," said number one. "The scarlet-fever room."

"It won't take long," said number two, wanting to be friendly. "We'll seal the door shut afterwards."

"You'll seal the door shut for how long?" I asked, thinking about bedding for the girls.

"Twenty-four hours," answered number one.

"These are the regulations," answered number two, still trying to not intimidate.

The sanitary officers entered the scarlet-fever room. They inspected its contents, pulled open the two beds, closed both the windows and then stood near the door. I stayed a safe distance behind them and watched as they lowered their air pistols in the direction of the beds. Yellow smoke billowed forth, smelling of sulfur. I moved further away. They kept at it until their guns were empty. My eyes stung.

The two officers backed into the hall and shut the door, sealing it tight with black tape. They covered even the keyhole. Then they turned around and found their way through the clouds of smoke to the front door.

"There is one more regulation," said number one, catching his breath. He reached into his bag and pulled out a death mask, a skull and cross bones, which he carefully unfolded.

"Usually," he explained, "when a case of scarlet fever is declared in the village, we come immediately and place this warning on the front door. It's a regulation."

"And then after the six weeks of quarantine, the family can take it off," said number two.

The two officers stood helplessly at the front door, with their skeleton's head dangling in mid-air between them.

"May I take it from you?" I suggested.

"*Si, si, Signora*," they replied in chorus, grateful to hand over the belated skull and bones.

Their mission was accomplished. Shouldering their air pistols, they bowed with ceremony and departed.

❧

The girls were still playing outside. Their baby brother was sleeping close by in his carriage. The apple trees on the hillside were bursting into spring. Church bells started to count to twelve. It was soon time for lunch.

I decided to leave the door to their room sealed tight and fix extra bedding for them in their brothers' room for the night. Twenty-four hours seemed short after six weeks.

Dr. Spock had warned, "Quarantine regulations vary a great deal in different localities." As proof, I put the skull and bones in our Italian souvenir album.

Countryside near Lago Maggiore

RATATOUILLE

—◀o▶—

Because I started making this dish with Il Nonno's gorgeous eggplants,
I never peeled them, or the zucchini, or the tomatoes.

2 eggplants (diced in ½ inch pieces)	*2 large onions (chopped)*
4 zucchini (diced in ½ inch pieces)	*2 cloves garlic (sliced)*
2 peppers (cut into small slices)	*4 large tomatoes (chopped)*
3 T. olive oil	*thyme, rosemary, laurel*
Salt and ground fresh pepper	*2 T. soy sauce (optional!)*

In a large heavy pot, sauté the onions and garlic in the olive oil, add the
peppers, stir, continue to sauté. Add eggplant, zuchinni, and tomatoes. Stir
in salt and pepper, soy sauce, and herbs. Simmer for 45 minutes. Taste and
adjust seasoning.

☞ *To serve hot with almost any dish, and then cold in salad the next day.*

Il Nonno

IL NONNO'S PINK ROSE BUSHES GREW AS TALL AS SMALL trees. They circled the pebbled terrace in front of the large white apartment house where we lived for close to five years, there on a hillside above the village of Comerio and Lago Maggiore. These were quiet years, except for a growing brood of children. Years of listening to church bells, of looking at the lake in the distance and, beyond, it Monte Rosa.

When we first met Il Nonno, it was his beaked nose I saw, jutting out from the sunken face. His shoulders sagged and his dark pants hung on black suspenders over a creased, yellowish shirt. He lifted the tip of his gray felt hat whenever he saw me and kept his words to himself.

Il Nonno—Grandfather Lucionni—moved into the white house when he could no longer live alone in the old farmhouse further down the hill. His son, with wife and daughter, made room for him. We lived above them, on the second floor, with our three young children. Often I worried about all the small footsteps above their heads but never did they mention it.

The lane going up the hill from the village was steep and cobbled with uneven stones. On one side a small stream found its way down over rocks, fallen branches, and clumps of nettles. On the other side there ran a stone wall and halfway up was the old farm, built around a courtyard with a small fountain in the middle. Near the top of the lane stood the large two-story white house. Beyond were thick woods with wild mushrooms and pheasants where hunters converged every September when the season opened.

At first, our three young children shied away from Il Nonno, as from a scarecrow stuck in a vegetable patch. They would play at the far end of the yard, keeping busy with their wagons, rag dolls and make-believe. From time to time they'd turn and steal a peek at him. And then return to their games, happy for one another and safely at a distance from Il Nonno.

Then one day in late October, after Peter, our oldest child, had come home from kindergarten, Il Nonno built a small wood fire in the middle of the pebbled terrace. He placed a blackened pan filled with chestnuts on top of the hot flames. I smelled the roasting chestnuts from the balcony of our apartment and went downstairs with the children. We gathered around to watch as Il Nonno shook the pan back and forth, and the skins popped open.

The chestnuts were hot and moist. The children tasted them and held out their hands for more. From then on, Peter hurried home each day from school, eager to find his new friend. Il Nonno would be waiting for him at the top of the lane. Sometimes he'd have more hot chestnuts waiting. Other times they would walk off hand in hand, past Il Nonno's vegetable garden, over the terraced hillside, down to the small reservoir, once used to irrigate the family farmlands. Below the farmlands rested the cemetery on the outskirts of the village.

Il Nonno grew eggplants a foot long, deep purple, and perfectly symmetrical. His tomatoes hung down low to the ground, ready to burst, and the green peppers gleamed in the midst of their dark leaves. Il Nonno taught Peter how to till the black clods of earth and plant the seeds, one by one, taking time to make sure they fell evenly. When the tomatoes were ripe and luscious, he would give Peter the most luscious ones to bring to us.

Il Nonno's granddaughter, Lucianna, taught at the local school. She was in her mid-twenties and still stayed close to home. Many evenings we'd sit together on the front steps, looking out over the red-tiled roofs of the village, the children playing in the last rays of sunlight. Lucianna would ask us about our impressions of their village, and then about our earlier homes in France and America. Her parents stayed on the steps, sitting with us, and listened. Il Nonno lingered close by, tending his rose trees. When the bells rang seven o'clock, we'd all go inside for supper.

Soon our fourth child was born. It was a noisy painful Italian birth. We baptized our new baby in the village church with many of the villagers attending. We were the only foreigners in the village and the parish had taken us in hand. Lucianna sat up front next to our children, her parents stayed further back, her mother with the women to the left, and her father with the men—the few that there were—to the right. Il Nonno stayed outside with the other men.

After the christening, we invited family and friends, along with Don Francesco, up the hill for a glass of wine, some cakes, and sugar-coated almonds. Tables were set out on the front terrace close to the rose trees, with fat tubs of ice to keep the bubbly Spumante cold. Il Nonno moved back and forth, greeting everyone. He was the patriarch and finally sat down near his son, looking like his shadow, shrunken in the sunlight.

The only other time that Il Nonno went near the church was on All Saints Day. He'd be dressed in black, except for his yellowish shirt with the creases ironed in, and waiting outside the open door. After Mass, he'd join the procession on its way to the cemetery, trailing behind from one tombstone to another. When he arrived at his family's tomb, he would stand in silence, forgetting to move on, until his son came and took him by the arm to lead him home.

The days and months turned into seasons. We lived outdoors, waiting for the first ripe tomatoes in the spring, sitting in the shade under the balcony in the hot summers, and smelling the roasted chestnuts in the fall. We let the church bells count the hours. At matins and vespers, they'd remind us to be still for a moment. When there were funerals, they tolled other memories. We'd watch from the terrace, waiting for the priest and mourners to leave the church and follow along in the direction of the cemetery at the bottom of the hillside. More than once Il Nonno would be there, staring out from a distant corner of the front yard, holding his felt hat close against his chest.

Il Nonno grew more and more gaunt. His clothes hung from his shoulders as from a bent wire hanger. He still waited for Peter each day but no longer did they go for long walks. The bright sun hurt his pale eyes, and even with a cane he was no longer steady on his feet. Peter helped him plant and water the vegetables. The roses, Il Nonno took care of alone. His hands knew the trees by heart, where to trim, where to prune, and where to let be.

I was expecting another baby for Easter. I continued with the daily errands and shopping, and when the weather grew warm, I'd be out of breath walking the two little ones back up the hill, over the bumpy cobblestones. Il Nonno would be standing near the rose bushes. He'd scowl as if to scold me for being out in the sun. Then he'd come hold the hands of the children. A smile would crack across his parched face.

Early one Sunday morning, it was time to go to the hospital. As I got into the car, I saw Lucianna and her parents watching from their kitchen window. And, further to the left, Il Nonno was watching from his bedroom. I waved and tightly hugged my bulging stomach.

It was once again a long birth and I appreciated the days of rest afterwards. We named the baby Lucie, a lovely little baby with rosy cheeks. Pierre came every day, often bringing along the children. One afternoon it was Lucianna's turn to come visit. She brought a deep pink rose from her grandfather. It was for the new baby. *"Per la piccola Lucia,"* Il Nonno had told her.

The last day at the hospital, Pierre arrived in the late afternoon after work. I was longing to be back home, with all our family together in the white house on the hillside. We drove up the narrow lane and parked near the border of rose trees. The children came running down the steps, crowding around as I carried little Lucie in my arms.

I looked up at the windows of the white house. For the first time, Il Nonno's shutters were closed. From down in the village, the funeral bells tolled.

Emilia's Petition

I MET EMILIA ONE SEPTEMBER AFTERNOON WHEN I WAS waiting at the corner in the village for the school bus. Our youngest child was toppling out of his pushcart and Katie, soon three, was pulling on my hand. Emilia joined our trio as if she belonged.

"Do you wait here every day?" she asked me in English.

"No. I take turns with my neighbor." I wondered where she came from, dressed up like a parrot, a red felt hat plopped on her head, a plaid bathrobe worn as a wraparound coat. She stood close and looked at me firmly.

"What days are your turn?" she asked.

"Mondays and Wednesdays."

"Good. I'll come and wait with you." She switched and spoke French, tapping me on the arm to show it was decided.

So each Monday and Wednesday Emilia would come and wait with us at the bottom of our lane for the school bus bringing Peter and Cecile home from the European School. Our village was halfway between the school and the research center at Ispra where Pierre worked.

"*Signora*, you are American?" she asked.

"Yes."

"And *il Signore Ingeniere* is French?" Her head bobbed up and down with each question.

"Yes."

She seemed to know all about us.

"*Bene*. Everyone else in the village is Italian. Now I will have a chance to speak English and French."

ȣʕ

One afternoon when the school bus was late, and we'd waited together for a long time, I invited Emilia up the hill for a cup of tea. As we walked up the lane, her red hat bounced with each step. I looked closely. An elastic band held it fast. The older children had asked me if I thought she had any hair underneath it. She turned and winked at me as if reading my thoughts.

"Emilia," I said, "where did you learn your French and English?"

"At school in Milano, before you were born." She nodded her head in agreement with herself. "It was during the war. The first war."

We arrived at the big white house on the hillside and climbed the stairs to our apartment. Emilia kept on her hat and bathrobe and entered the living room, stopping in front of the bookshelves and squinting at the titles.

"Emilia, do you read in English?"

"Yes."

"And in French?"

"Yes. And in Chinese and Japanese." She gazed out the window to the village and the old church and the cemetery.

"Where did you learn Chinese and Japanese?"

"In China, during the second war."

❧

Emilia told me she had left Italy when she was forty, just before the Second World War, to go marry someone whom she'd never met, an Italian living halfway around the world in China. She was working in Milan for Kodak, and he was working in Port Arthur for Kodak.

"He liked the way I wrote business letters."

"And so?"

"And so he wrote and asked me to come marry him."

"You took off alone for China without ever having seen him?"

"Yes. It was my last chance. I was almost forty. I arrived early one Saturday morning with my small traveling bag. I came back some ten years later with the same bag." She blinked both eyes. "He met me at the boat and had a missionary priest waiting to marry us. On Monday morning, I was typing business letters in China instead of in Italy."

"Did you fall in love?"

"Heavens no! We stayed together through the war and that was enough. When we came back to Italy, he wanted to go to an old folks' home." She shook her head. "I said no. I knew it would kill me. But he insisted and, sure enough, it killed him. I was alone at his burial, alone with the priest from the old folks' home."

She stopped talking. She had run out like a dizzy top, even her red hat sat still, slanting a bit to one side.

One Sunday, when I invited her to our midday meal, a roasted chicken with tomatoes from the garden, she arrived carrying a large manila envelope under her arm.

"This is my petition. I want you and *il Signore Ingeniere* to sign it."

I asked her what it was about.

"It's about letting dead folk be cremated," she said, looking at me intently. "Italy is too chock-full of old bones." She spread out her petition on the Sunday table. It was written in Latin. There were two pages of signatures.

"But why is it in Latin?"

"It looks better. Everyone in the village thinks it's Catholic if it's in Latin."

Emilia explained that every year she sent her petition to the Italian government in Rome. And every year she collected about one hundred signatures, most of them the same as the year before.

"I won't give up," she said, with a chuckle, "not until they've changed the law."

Our children asked her one day to take off her hat. She obliged and pulled off the hat and the elastic. On the top of her head crouched a disheveled gray bun, with more hairpins than hair.

"I used to have long, thick black hair," she told them. "When I was living in China, I wore it pulled back in a fat pigtail. I must have pulled it too tight for it started to fall out. It came out by the handful."

Our children listened in dismay.

"But never you mind," she said. "Look here, while I was there, I learned how to slant my eyes."

We all looked. It was true. Emilia knew how to slant her eyes.

"How do you do it?" asked Peter.

"First you must go to China," she replied. And she plopped her red hat back on her head, becoming once again the Emilia we knew.

৵

It was my husband who persuaded her one day to take off her plaid bathrobe which she continued to wear on top of her dress.

"Emilia," he said, "I want to see you with just your dress, without the bathrobe."

"Ah, you Frenchmen!" And she took off her bathrobe and showed us a plain, gray woolen dress.

"It becomes you Emilia," Pierre said. "It's the color of your hair."

She took off her hat once more and tried to pat her hair in place. Pierre was right. I could imagine how she looked when she first arrived in China after traveling halfway around the world.

"You know," she confided, "I do wish it had been the French correspondent who asked me to marry him instead of the Italian." She opened wide her black eyes and smiled.

We listened.

"He was ever so attractive. We lent one another books. We studied Chinese and Japanese together in the evening." She looked away, far out the window, beyond the village, beyond the lake. Something had stopped her, there in the middle of her story.

"And then?" we asked.

"And then he was called back to Paris at the end of the war. I never heard from him again." She shook her head and closed her eyes.

ৈৄ

Little by little we got to know Emilia. We invited her for roast chicken every Sunday. She'd arrive at our front door with a tin of English tea biscuits. The cookies lasted most of the week. The tins lasted much longer. We kept them for dominos, marbles, and buttons, Emilia's biscuit tins.

The children continued to prefer her with her plaid bathrobe and red felt hat. The straggly bun of hairpins made them uneasy. She'd slant her eyes for them while she wore her hat. They said that was how she looked the best.

ৈৄ

One time, instead of the round tin of English tea biscuits, she brought a large rectangular gift-wrapped box.

"Something special for the children."

It was the game Monopoly in Italian. From then on after dinner, she'd sit down on the balcony and play Monopoly with them.

If ever Pierre or I would watch, she'd send us away. "It's time you two had a moment alone. Now off with you, but no nonsense, no fooling around, you have more than enough children as it is."

❧

One Sunday, when she was leaving, a rainstorm broke and we drove her down the hill to the village. She didn't want us to come to her door. Then the following Sunday she told me I could come, if I wanted, but alone. "There's barely room for me."

We walked down the lane. Emilia was quiet. I could hear the little brook to our left rippling over the stones and fallen branches. Emilia kept stealing sideways glances at me. We crossed the street and went into the village, down past the bakery and the church.

Her house was on a little alley and up a few wooden steps. She opened her door and let me in. There was one small room. In the far corner stood a washstand and a table with an electric plate; that was her kitchen. Half under the sink was an old fashioned bathtub. She heated the water in the kettle. The toilet was outside in the back.

In the near corner was her bed, piled high with blankets and a brightly embroidered silk spread on top. The spread, she said, was the only souvenir she brought back from China—red and blue winged birds against gold-threaded sunlight. Against the walls, shelves were stacked high with books—old books, some with leather bindings. I wished later that I had looked at the titles, remembering the way she had looked at ours.

ॐ

We signed Emilia's petition four years in a row. But the Italian government wasn't ready to budge. They wanted everyone buried and accounted for.

Come spring of our fourth year, it was time for us to move on. Pierre was leaving his work in Italy.

Emilia came for one last Sunday dinner. We walked up the hill together after church. Her hat was askew, and we were not able to cheer her up.

The older children asked her to play Monopoly. They got out the game, the cards in Italian, and opened it on the table outside on the balcony. But Emilia's heart was no longer there. She said it was best she be on her way.

We hugged her and promised we'd come back.

She sighed.

"We'll come back and sign your petition," we said.

"You'll see," she said, "one day they'll give in."

And off she went, without turning around, down the lane across the street, and into the village.

ॐ

Our first letter came back unopened. The envelope was dirty and torn. The word, "*deceduta*" was scribbled over her name.

A year later, when we returned to Italy, we learned that the village had buried Emilia in their cemetery. We found her gravestone and stood in front of it for a long time, crying hard and trying to say goodbye.

Years later, when the Italian government finally changed the law to allow for cremation, I thought I heard her groan. Or did she chuckle?

SUNDAY ROAST CHICKEN

—◆o►—

1 medium to large roasting chicken (cleaned and rinsed)	2 medium onions
6 medium tomatoes	2 garlic cloves
4 T. olive oil	salt and ground pepper
12 medium mushrooms	thyme, rosemary, basil
	3 T. soy sauce

Preheat oven to hot, 400 F.

Place chicken in roasting pan, spread with 3 T. olive oil, 2 T. soy sauce, herbs (fresh if possible), and pepper (very little salt is needed when soy sauce is used). Roast in hot oven for 15 minutes, baste, then reduce to 375.

Add tomatoes and onions coarsely chopped and mixed together with 1 T. olive oil, 1 T. soy and more herbs.

Roast for another 45 minutes, basting several times. If there is not enough liquid from the tomatoes, add water as needed. Stir mushrooms cut in quarters into tomatoes and onions during the last 15 minutes of roasting time.

☞ *The chicken should be golden brown, and the tomatoes and onions almost pureed to make a good gravy.*

SWITZERLAND
1969 – 1975

Le Lac de Genève

Swiss Scaffolds

WE MOVED TO GENEVA IN 1970 WHEN SWITZERLAND WAS getting ready to decide the fate of its foreigners. A politician from Zurich, named Herr Schwarzenbach, was initiating a referendum which would drastically limit the number of *Ausländer* living in the country.

The Swiss government consults its citizens regularly through referendums, and its citizens choose the issues through petitions. We didn't know about Herr Schwarzenbach or about his inhospitable referendum when Pierre accepted a new job with an international computer company in Geneva.

We arrived from Italy where the number of foreigners was unlimited, as was the number of children. With five young ones in tow, we realized rapidly that such large families were very un-Swiss. When we trotted around the city streets in search of an apartment, people would stop and stare at our brood. Only the swans at the lakeside had as many offspring, and the baby swans followed in single file.

Housing, we learned, was also limited in Geneva. Real estate agents would shake their heads in disbelief. Sometimes in sympathy one of them would say, "*Hélas, Madame...*" We finally found a three-bedroom apartment on the fifth floor of a brand new building near the airport. The real estate man assured us that the walls were soundproof against the noise of planes and, he added, the noise of children.

Scaffolds surrounded the building. Our children moved into the three bedrooms. Pierre and I moved into the dining room, along with the piano. The apartment had windows to the east and the Alps, and windows to the west and the Jura mountains. From inside we didn't see the scaffolds but we saw the workmen. They'd wave to one another across the apartment. They, too, had arrived from Italy. Soon they started to wave to the children. "*Ciao, ciao!*"

Inside the building, we never saw anyone. The halls were empty, the elevator was empty. We were beginning to wonder if we were maybe the only people in the whole building. Then one morning when Pierre was going out the main front door to the street, a pink nightgown floated down into his arms. He looked up the ten floors behind all the scaffolds, and somewhere near the top a woman was waving to him to wait. He stood at the door, holding the pink nightgown in his arms, until her husband arrived to retrieve it. They were our first acquaintances in the building. They, too, were foreigners. She was Belgian, he was Danish.

ॐ

Each apartment came with a small cellar with massive armored doors that doubled as an air-raid shelter, mandatory in all new dwellings in Geneva. The norms for the atomic shelters were very precise and corresponded to the number of bedrooms in each apartment. Our three bedrooms entitled us to a shelter for a family of four. The concierge, who was also Italian and delighted to see so many children—*"Tanti bambini, Signora!"*—tried to find us a second shelter, but there were no extras. *"Peccato, Signora, peccato."*

With each shelter came a small red book about civil defense, published by the Federal Justice Department. It was written that all citizens were invited to take the necessary measures for their own protection in case of armed conflict. One of the measures stated that it was the responsibility of the housewife to keep two months of reserves for each member of the family in case of an emergency. We multiplied by seven and realized there wouldn't be room in the shelter for both the reserves and us. We forgot about the reserves and filled the shelter with skis in the summer and bicycles in the winter.

The underground garages were calculated as tightly as the cellars. When we squeezed in our Peugeot station wagon, we could barely open the doors. We learned to first let everyone out, then drive the car into the garage as close as possible to the far side so the driver could get out on the other side. Obviously, there was no allowance for pregnant drivers, but I wasn't yet thinking of having another child.

Even at church, we were flagrantly too many and always ushered to the rows in the back. Five children all together would certainly disturb the service. It was only when Peter became an altar boy that we were allowed to sit closer to the front. There was one less child to make noise.

Solely the local grade school was happy to see so many of us. In order to obtain new classrooms and new teachers, a school had to have a certain enrollment. The arrival of our children did the trick. The school got two new classrooms and two new teachers. I hoped there might be the same quotas and magic in order to have a school cafeteria. But I was told that children were supposed to go home in the middle of the day to rest— hence the extra-long two-and-a-half–hour lunch break.

So home they came every day for two and a half hours at lunchtime. We went for piano lessons one day and swimming lessons another. The other days we practiced piano and played outside. When I finally walked them back to school and returned home to put the youngest to nap, I'd fall fast asleep myself, sometimes until it was time to go fetch them.

I missed Italy, I missed the large white house on the hill, I missed the church bells, I missed the friendly neighbors. We decided to give a house-warming party, or rather a building-warming party. Our children put invitations in all the mailboxes in the front lobby. To our surprise, most of the apartments were occupied and everyone came.

I had wanted to make name tags, with the floor and apartment number of each guest, but Pierre said it was not the sort of thing the Swiss would appreciate. I didn't think the French would either.

Everyone said it was a fine party, *"C'était très gentil de nous inviter."* It was very nice to invite them but no one else offered to give another "fine party" The only people we saw again were the people on the tenth floor, the Belgian woman with the pink nightgown and her Danish husband.

The first days of summer brought along the dreaded referendum that Herr Schwarzenbach had initiated. All over the city, ominous posters warned that a full one-third of the population in Geneva was foreign. The posters also warned that the same one-third was very prolific. We had grown accustomed to our condition—foreign and prolific. I was no longer hiding children behind my back. In fact our five children had learned to stand in single file even in the elevator.

As the vote approached, there were rumblings in the air, passions were aroused. The outcome was uncertain. As foreigners, we sought out one another's company. We wondered if the Swiss would really tell us to leave. Finally the votes were counted. Herr Schwarzenbach lost. Switzerland liked its foreigners, and Geneva, of all the twenty-five cantons, liked its foreigners the best.

It was after the vote that the Italian workmen started to dismantle the scaffolds that were still in place. They took down one level after the other. Soon window boxes of red geraniums appeared, starting from the top floor and continuing down.

When the scaffolds were carted off and the apartments stood on their own, the workmen came to our front door to say goodbye. We were here to stay, so were they. "*Arrivederci!*"

In Line

IT'S THE GRAND OPENING OF THE FIRST SHOPPING CENTER in Switzerland. And it's close to Christmastime. I leave the car in the immense parking lot below, and up we go on brand new escalators.

"Please, stay in line." Five children in order of age behind their mom. There are red balloons for all of them. It's hard to hold on to one another. The shops are decorated with sprays of evergreens and ribbons, tinsel and lights. The shop windows are filled with chocolates, ski sweaters, and Swiss music boxes.

"Please, hold on tight to each other." We are jiggled by the crowds. Christmas carols fill the air. "Silent Night," "Mon Beau Sapin." I stop to watch automated teddy bears clap their hands and beat on drums. The music stops for an announcement. "Three-year old Lucie is looking for her mother."

In such dazzle, lines don't work.

Our Apartment Building, Geneva

"I'm Here"

MY HUSBAND WAVES GOODBYE AS HE GOES OUT THE apartment door. I call after him, "Have a good day. I love you." Does he hear me, in the midst of five children, all of us sitting around the kitchen table? The children hardly raise their heads. They're used to their father going off to work and their mother staying home.

It's Thursday, the day when there is no school in Geneva, when the fathers are at work and the mothers are at home, taking care of the children. This particular Thursday instead of taking them to their morning dance lessons for the girls and judo for the boys, I am taking them to the doctor's for their annual check-up, then home for a birthday luncheon for number three, then on to their afternoon music lessons.

The Swiss pediatrician tried to discourage my bringing the five at one time, worrying about his waiting room where the rule apparently was one mother, one child. Now he just tries to keep track.

"Okay, young fellow, your turn," he says to seven-year-old Christopher. "Jump right up on the bed."

Chris obeys, but he's rather pudgy and misses the top of the bed, tumbling down on the tiled floor and biting his tongue. There is a crunching sound and blood spouts forth.

"*Mon Dieu!*" "My God!" gasps the doctor, setting Chris straight on a stool and stuffing cotton into the child's mouth. "Tongues are tricky. They can hemorrhage," he says nodding his bald head and wiping off his glasses. "Sometimes they have to be stitched. If it's still bleeding this afternoon, bring the young fellow to me at the hospital."

Chris is looking up at me. His mother will take care of him.

ॐ

It isn't until we are all in the elevator, going up the five floors that I realize I have locked us out of the apartment.

"Kids, guess what. I forgot the key inside the apartment."

"Come on, Mom, you're teasing," says someone.

"I am not teasing."

"But my birthday party," says Katie, "Mom, you're forgetting my party."

"No, I am not forgetting. Don't worry, you'll have your party, we'll find a way." Squeezed into the elevator, the five kids are all staring at me. I narrow my eyes to think better. "Maybe Antonio, the concierge, has an extra key." And back down we go the five floors.

Antonio greets us warmly. He is Italian and loves children, and women.

"*Si, Signora*, I will open your door."

"But, Antonio, do you have a key?"

"No *Signora*, but I will climb over the balcony." And off he goes toward the elevator. We run along after him. One of the kids says something about whether their father would do the same.

"Antonio, I do not want you to climb over the balcony. I will telephone my husband."

"No, *Signora*, do not disturb you husband. Antonio is happy to help you."

On the fifth floor landing, there is a small balcony next to ours. Antonio disappears out of sight. I try to hold on to as many children as possible. "Stay here," I call out, and before I make sure they are all there, Antonio has climbed over the balcony and is opening our front door from the inside.

He bows gallantly, "*Signora, prego*, come in."

Katie's birthday guests start to arrive. I quickly call my husband's office. He is out, somewhere at a business luncheon. His secretary doesn't know when he will be back.

Five little girls arrive, plus my five, that makes ten. The table was set the night before: pink paper tablecloth, pink napkins, pink party favors. I serve French fries and frankfurters. And my five-times-a-year birthday cake. A recipe from *Pomme d'Api*, the monthly children's magazine, it takes five minutes to make.

Later, as the mothers come to pick up their little girls, I smile and say how happy I was to have their children.

"You must be used to having so many," says one mother, looking around at all the heads.

"Yes, probably so," I answer.

"But you can't imagine," says another, "how lonely I was without my little Genevieve for lunch today."

"No, probably not."

Christopher brings me out of my reverie. His tongue is still bleeding. I telephone the doctor. The older children will have to go to their music lessons alone, and I will take the two youngest to the hospital.

৯

Christopher will have a general anesthetic, the operating room is ready, and within an hour it will all be over. A nurse leads us into a small room where Chris puts on a white hospital gown and lays down on a white bed. His little sister won't let go of my hand. I tell them both everything will be all right. The nurse wheels Chris away.

We go to the lounge and I find a telephone booth. This time my husband answers. I explain where we are.

"What's the doctor say?"

"It will all be over in an hour."

"Do you want me to come?"

"No." I try to stop crying.

"Then I better go home to check on the others." He waits for me to say something. "Are you all right?"

"Yes, I'm all right." I pause. "I was wondering, would you climb over a balcony for me?"

"I guess so. Why?"

I start to tell him about what happened, about Christopher biting his tongue, about my locking us out, about Antonio climbing the balcony, but he says I should wait and tell him later.

I sit down near my youngest child who has already curled up in an armchair and is sound asleep. It is already late in the afternoon and everything is quiet. My head nods. The lights become very bright. I am in the operating room. I can see Christopher lying on the operating table. There are many doctors and nurses all dressed in white. They don't see me. My children are also there, spread out around the room. They are looking for me. They don't see me either. I try to tell them I am there, but they don't hear me. In the distance someone is waving. It is my husband. He is climbing over the balcony and into the room.

"*Madame,*" says the voice of the pediatrician. "Your son is here. The operation is over and the young fellow is fine." The lights are once again dim. I stand up. Chris is resting on the bed in front of me. A nurse is waiting to wheel him to the car.

He opens his eyes and looks for me. "Mom, are you there?"

I nod. "Yes, I'm here."

GATEAU POMME D'API

—◄o►—

This being an easy recipe for children, the given instructions
call for using the yogurt container as a measure. In Europe the
yogurt 'pots' are fairly standard, coming to ½ of a cup.

½ cup plain yogurt	¼ cup oil (sunflower/peanut)
1½ cups flour	2 eggs
1 cup sugar	2 teaspoons baking powder

Preheat the oven to 350 F.

In a big bowl, pour the yogurt, flower, sugar, oil, eggs and baking powder.
Mix well everything together. Butter a cake pan. Pour in the mixture and
cook in a moderate oven for 45 minutes.

☞ *Top with Nutella or melted chocolate. Put a few candles, Happy Birthday!*

The Straw Chair, Saigon

The Straw Chair

DANIEL WAS TWO YEARS OLD WHEN HE CAME TO US. WE were waiting at the airport. We were waiting and wondering whether he would ever really arrive, whether he would ever really come home with us.

One year earlier, we wrote to a distant aunt on my husband's side, a Benedictine sister living in Saigon. We asked if she knew of a war orphan who needed a family. We had moved into a house of our own with a large yard on a quiet street. We had room for another child.

I still remember when I received her answer. As I tore open the envelope, a photo fell out, a small black and white photo of one-year-old Daniel. He looked the size of a newborn baby, with a large head and large dark eyes. He was sitting in a small straw chair, leaning to one side, as if he might slide out of it.

The Benedictine sister wrote that the mother had entrusted her with the baby before she moved on with a group of Cambodian refugees. The father, probably an American soldier, had disappeared. The very same morning that my letter arrived, the sister received the first satisfactory bill of health for Daniel, after months of intensive medical care.

Pierre and I spoke to each one of our children about welcoming a new baby into our family. Peter, then thirteen, was sitting in the kitchen, looking at the world map on the wall. "You know, Mom, I was just looking at the map," he said, "and wondering if we could do something like that."

The next two, both girls, were then eleven and nine. "Another baby? From far away?" they asked. "Can't we have two? Please! One for each of us. "

The two youngest, Christopher and Lucie, aged six and three, didn't care where their new little brother was coming from. They knew somehow they'd be the closest.

So we waited together, sharing each new letter. At Christmas we received a second photo. Daniel was standing up this time. We recognized the same little straw chair. He was holding on to it with both hands. We put the photo in the middle of the Christmas tree in our front hall. Daniel was to be the family's forever gift.

Our two youngest moved in together, leaving the smaller bedroom for their new little brother. We brought down the white wooden crib from the attic and repainted it. We also brought down the box of baby clothes. Each child picked out one of their favorite stuffed animals and put it on Daniel's bed.

All we knew about Daniel was that he was living in an orphanage on the outskirts of Saigon, along with hundreds of other refugee children. I never asked about anything else—how big he was, what he ate, where he slept, how he played, what he spoke. It just seemed like he would be one of us, that once he was in our family, he would grow up like his brothers and sisters.

It took us six months to complete the legal papers for adoption in Saigon. The judgment was made in January. Then we had to obtain a visa for Daniel to enter Switzerland. The Swiss authorities questioned us at length.

"Madame, have you thought this all through?" they asked.

"Yes," I answered.

"Then if you really want another child, why don't you have one of your own? We already have too many foreigners in Switzerland."

I respectfully explained that we ourselves were foreigners and that Daniel was already one of us.

Finally everything was ready. Daniel had a Vietnamese passport and a Swiss visa. He could come to us. Now we had to find transportation. This was back in 1974. The Viet Cong was encircling Saigon. The war was at its worst. Very few planes were coming in or going out. We learned that Air France was flying a group of orphans to Paris almost every week. We put Daniel on the list. The Benedictine sister wrote that she would get him to the airport.

Week after week we waited, thinking the next time it would be his turn. Each day the children came home from school, hoping to learn that their little brother was on his way. And each day there was still no news.

Their teachers didn't know what to make of all their excitement. Our children tried to explain. Yes, they were going to have a new brother. Yes, he would be two years old. Of course, he would be their brother. Of course, they would love him.

Then we received the telegram: "Daniel arriving Friday, April 26, noon, Air France #404." It was Thursday, April 25. That evening we prayed—all of us together—harder than ever.

Pierre flew to Paris to wait for him. His brothers and sisters went to school. I stayed home and counted the minutes.

When the phone rang, I knew it was Pierre.

"I have news," he said.

"Yes?"

"Unfortunately the plane's been delayed. It had to stop for repairs..."

I don't remember what else he said. Only that he would call back as soon as he learned something more.

The children came home for lunch. They had been excused for the afternoon and were expecting to drive to the airport. I told them it was not yet time.

"What do you mean not yet time?" asked Peter.

"The plane had to stop somewhere," I answered.

"What happened?" asked another.

"And Daniel, where is he?"

"Is he all right?"

"When will he come?"

I answered as best I could, trying to reassure them, and at the same time reassure myself. I told them their little brother was safe and would soon be with us.

I couldn't send them back to school, each child alone in his class wondering all afternoon whether Daniel would ever arrive. So we stayed together and tried to pass the time as best we could. When the phone rang a second time, the children raced ahead and then stood back to let me answer. I picked up the phone and listened.

"This time there's good news," said my husband.

"Yes?"

"His plane will land in less than an hour," he continued. "That means that I should be able to make the next flight to Geneva."

"With Daniel?"

"With Daniel."

The last hours passed. We got into the car, and somehow I drove to the airport. Was it my heart, or was it really the car, skidding all the way? I knew the streets well yet everything looked different. I was going into uncharted land.

We hurried into the terminal. The flight from Paris had just landed. Crowding behind the wide glass window, we looked at the far end of the luggage hall, where the passengers were arriving through the gate. The five children positioned themselves up front and pressed their faces flat against the glass. I stood behind, suddenly afraid.

I saw my husband. He was taller than the other passengers. He was carrying Daniel in his arms and walking in our direction.

"I see him! Look, I see Daddy!" shouted Cecile.

"He's there. He's there!"

"Where? Where is he?" asked the youngest.

"There. And he's got Daniel."

"Mom, do you see them?" asked Peter. He turned and looked at me. I didn't have time to hide the tears.

We went to the arrival gate. My husband and Daniel were among the first. They had no baggage, just each other—father and son. Pierre waved to us and put Daniel down, trying to stand him on his feet.

But Daniel didn't know how to stand on his own. The straw chair, the little straw chair he was holding on to in the photo, was back in Saigon. He fell forward and hit his head on tile floor. And then, so far from home, frozen with fear, he hit once more against the cold hard floor of the airport.

We picked him up and carried him home in our arms.

Welcoming Daniel

His Story, Our Story

THE DAY DANIEL CAME TO US FROM SAIGON, EVERYTHING was new to him. He watched us and we watched him.

His first smile came the second day, when he was sitting in the bathtub, with the rest of us kneeling around him. He stared up at us with big dark eyes. Lucie, closest in age, splashed him just a little. He looked at her in surprise. He picked up his hand and tapped lightly the top of the water. Drops of water caught the light. He did it again, the drops sprinkled in a rainbow. Then he looked back at Lucie and with a big smile he splashed her back.

We had no common language to help us understand one another. Daniel had heard only Vietnamese and wasn't speaking. Instead he hummed, a nasal chanting hum, like a litany or a lullaby, over and over. We stopped using English and only spoke French to help him with just one new language. It was after many months that he said his first word, *Maman*, and very soon *Papa*. Still today the words are an immense pledge of trust.

He slept very little those first months in the white wooden crib high off the floor, with bars on all sides. Only later did I learn from the Benedictine sister, that at the orphanage he slept on a mat on the floor in the middle of lots of other children. Evening after evening, he cried, and Pierre or I would sit near him, holding his hand until he fell asleep. And when a few hours later he'd wake up screaming, his little body tight with fear, I'd take him in my arms and rock him back to sleep.

For a long time he couldn't stand up alone. Then he had trouble walking and would reach out for the nearest person's hand. Only in the summer, two months after his arrival, when we were at the seaside in France, did we discover why. We were walking along the beach on the wet sand, when we noticed that his two footprints were not the same. On one side, there were no heel marks, only toe marks. Watching him closely from behind, we saw that one leg was a little shorter than the other, a sequel to the polio he had as a small child in Vietnam. He did not walk on both heels. He still doesn't but he's learned to run, play soccer and tennis, and race on skis.

His brothers and sisters took him in tow. Whatever they did, he wanted to do. Our upright piano was in the downstairs hall, and the children would practice one after another. Daniel would sit close by and listen. If ever one of us would make too much noise close by, he would put his finger on his lips and go "*chut!*" Soon his brothers and sisters were teaching him to play. He'd touch just one key and then he would again put his finger to his lips and say "*chut!*"

At mealtimes it was often his oldest sister, Cecile, who fed him. Daniel at first liked only rice. We had to persuade him to like most everything else. We'd mix carrots into his rice, chicken into his rice, even applesauce and bananas. Never would he let one small grain fall from the spoon and be lost. Instead he would stop eating, look for the grain, pick it up, put it in his mouth, lick each finger, and then open his mouth for another spoonful.

His next oldest sister was feeding him the day he first tasted ice cream. We were sitting around the dining room table and enjoying lemon sorbet for dessert. Daniel was watching us from his high chair. Katie offered him a taste. He tried and wrinkled up his face, puckering his lips, squeezing shut his eyes. Then he pulled on her hand to try again. After a few more tries, a few more times wrinkling his nose, lemon sorbet became a favorite.

He always had an audience around him. At the school fair in June, Christopher and Lucie took him on the merry-go-round. They gave him a ticket and sat him on a small white horse. When the merry-go-round started to turn, Daniel held on with one hand and kept the ticket in the other. But when his horse started to go up and down, he put the ticket in his mouth and gripped the horse with both his hands. He held on tight until the music stopped, and his brother and sister loosened his arms from around the horse's neck.

At the swimming pool, he watched his brothers and sisters jump from the board into the water and come back up, waving to him. One day Peter took his hand and walked him to the end of the board. They jumped together. Soon Daniel was going out on the board alone and jumping into the middle of the deep water. He wasn't afraid as long as Peter was waiting for him below. He'd stand there, in his bright yellow bathing trunks, at the end of the board. When Peter said, "Ready? Jump!" he jumped.

Daniel has always been close to his brothers and sisters. They were his and he was theirs. In our family we take lots of photographs. There are rows of albums, lined up on the bottom bookshelf in the front hall. Each child has his own album, and there are the family albums, one for each year.

One afternoon Daniel was looking at the beginning pages in his album. The first photo shows him sitting on the front hood of a 2CV that the Benedictine sister borrowed to drive him to the airport in Saigon, his last day in Vietnam. The next picture shows him playing on the floor of his small bedroom with his new youngest brother and sister, a few days after his arrival in Geneva. He looked for a long time at each photo.

Then he took out another album. It was his oldest sister's album. On the first page he saw a picture of her as a baby. He looked up and asked her where she was born.

"Brussels," she said, "in another country."

"Is it far away?" he asked.

"Yes, it's far away."

"Did you also come on a plane?"

I don't remember what his sister answered. It was a difficult question.

How far is far away? Vietnam, Belgium, Switzerland? Italy, France, America?

Daniel was growing up with his sisters and brothers. His story was becoming our story.

Once a Year

ONCE A YEAR I PULL FROM MY RECIPE BOX THE CARD titled Anna's Christmas Stollen. It is the most bespattered of all the recipes, spattered with spice and love.

Anna was my mother's mother who sailed to America at the turn of the twentieth century, sixteen years old, alone, with the scents of Switzerland tucked away beneath her woolen cape. Her life was compressed into half a century. Married to a German immigrant, she had one daughter, my mother. Widowed very young, she came to live with us when she was ill. She passed away quickly but her love and grace remained. As did her Christmas stollen recipe, with its flavor and fragrance.

As a child, I remember when each year a few nights before Christmas, my mother would take out Anna's recipe card. The list of ingredients ran down both sides: flour, milk, eggs, sugar, butter, yeast on one side, and then slivered almonds, candied orange and lemon peel, dried raisins, and cinnamon on the other. After Mother mixed everything together and kneaded the dough well, she set the loaf aside for one entire night to

117

let it rise. The scent of yeast, almonds, cinnamon, and brandy filled the house, the scent of spice and love.

"It smells like Christmas," I used to say.

Then in the morning, Mother baked the large loaf. The first slices, hot and crumbly, were always the best. The raisins almost burned my lips. It was the almonds I liked the most, their crunchiness and bittersweet taste.

Sixty years after Anna sailed across the ocean, it was my turn to sail back. I brought much of my childhood with me, in souvenirs and memories. Before I left, I copied several of my mother's recipes. Anna's Christmas Stollen was coming home.

I found a small card box, about the size of my mother's, and covered it with a similar red and white checkered cloth. It traveled with me from country to country. I added recipes from France and Belgium, from Italy and Switzerland. I switched from tablespoons to decigrams, from cups to deciliters, and from fahrenheit to centigrade. But the recipe for Anna's Christmas Stollen stayed the same and got more and more spattered.

Here in Switzerland, the red and white box sits in the cupboard near the stove. It's filled tight with recipes, a travel log of where we've lived. Some of the recipes have dates and places marked on them, each one bringing back a memory.

A few nights before Christmas, we have a stollen night. It is the part of our Christmas festivity that did not change as we moved around Europe, adopting different customs from each country. In France I celebrated my first *réveillon*, the Christmas feast after midnight Mass, with hot chocolate and mandarin oranges, and little gifts in our shoes placed in front of the very large crèche. We continued the tradition but added bubbly wine and put our presents under the Christmas tree, with a smaller crèche close by.

In Belgium we added the feast day of Saint Nicholas, December 6. Pierre dressed up as Saint Nicholas and arrived with his bag of gifts for good children, and his bag of switches for naughty children. We then proceeded to celebrate with gifts once again at Christmas, and no switches.

In Italy we joined our Italian neighbors in their Epiphany parties, January 6, with a third round of gifts. And with *la Torta dei Re Maghi*, the King's Cake, with a little figure hidden inside the sweet round cake. Whoever discovered it was crowned king for the occasion. By this time our children were completely spoiled and thought they were all kings, or at least princes and princesses.

Back to our stollen night. Once all the ingredients are assembled, the children gather around the kitchen table, the smaller ones kneeling on stools, each with a large bowl. They have washed their hands and are ready to stir the flour and sugar into the warm milk and butter mixture. Then the eggs, the sticky citrus fruit, the raisins, and the almonds. I add brandy—with a swallow for the father—as they kneed and shape the dough into same-sized loaves.

Each year we make more and more loaves, doubling the recipe, tripling, up to fifteen or twenty loaves to share with our neighbors and friends. We sprinkle each loaf with sugar and cinnamon, and as they start to rise, the scent fills the house.

"It smells like Christmas," the children say.

I bake the loaves early in the morning. The first slices are warm and delicious, even if they crumble. The house wakes up. Children and grandchildren come down to the kitchen to taste. Hot, sweet crumbs of stollen stick to their fingers.

I close my eyes and smell the scent of spice and love.

ANNA'S CHRISTMAS STOLLEN

—◄o►—

2 cups milk	2 cups yellow raisins
1 cup sugar	2 cups slivered almonds
2 teaspoons salt	1 cup diced candied fruit (lemon &
1½ cups butter	orange peel, cherries, pineapple)
2 ounces fresh yeast	2 teaspoons almond extract
8 cups flour	2 ounces brandy
4 beaten eggs	

Scald milk; add sugar, salt, butter, and cool. Crumble in yeast with 2 cups of the flour; let rise (2 hours).

Add rest of flour, plus eggs, raisins, almonds, fruit, extract and brandy. Knead well and form either one very large loaf or four bread-size loaves. Brush loaves with melted butter and sprinkle with sugar and cinnamon. Let rise 12 hours.

Bake in moderate oven (350 F) for 1 hour for large loaf, 40 minutes for smaller loaves.

☞ *When cool, wrap and store in refrigerator to keep moist.*

The Water Jug

The Water Jug

IN OUR KITCHEN THERE IS AN OLD ROUND TABLE OF DARK walnut. On the table there is an earthenware jug, the color of moist gray clay. It looks as sturdy as the table. Yet at the bottom of the jug, a very fine vein is working its way upward through the rings of clay, etching itself slowly into the smooth surface.

Late one afternoon a close friend, a Dutch woman who makes pottery, turned the jug around in her hands.

"The water jug has a story of its own," I said. "Do you know the monastery on top of the Voirons mountains, northeast of Geneva, just over the border in France?"

"No," she said. "I know the mountains. I've gone hiking there, close to the top, but I never stopped at the monastery."

I told her about the Monastic Sisters of Bethlehem, a fairly recent religious community, who live there and how welcoming they are when I go up for an afternoon or for a whole weekend.

"The sisters make pottery for their livelihood. That's where I bought the water jug many years ago."

&

It was summertime. Pierre was working at his office in downtown Geneva, the children were staying with their grandparents. In early morning I drove up the mountain to the old monastery. The road climbs steeply, cutting through forests of tall pine trees, leaving the fields far below. At the end of the road, near the top of the mountain, a wooden gate welcomes the visitor to the religious community, named Bethlehem which in Hebrew means House of Bread. Beyond the wooden gate, the visitor is asked to remain in silence.

I joined the sisters in the small chapel adjacent to the ancient refectory. They were sitting in a semicircle on small wooden prayer benches. Oil lamps illumined the icons on either side of the stone altar. A monk, wearing the same long white prayer robes as the sisters, was celebrating Mass. I settled myself on a prayer bench and followed the liturgy. We came together around the altar for the Eucharist, to share the bread and wine. At the end of Mass there was a long moment of silent prayer.

Afterwards I went with the sisters to the refectory for the noonday meal. We sat at long tables and ate in silence. Before going outside, I helped clear off the tables and worked side by side with some of the sisters in the kitchen to wash and dry the dishes. Then I went to find a place to rest on the mountain slope facing Mont Blanc. The summit of the mountain rose above the layer of clouds, brilliant white in the immense blue sky.

Once a good-hearted monk, a Dominican—the one who welcomed me into the Catholic Church—told me that prayer and rest were much the same thing. So I rested and let myself fall asleep, lying there in the high grass on the side of the mountain. The bell for vespers woke me. I returned to the chapel full of stillness and warmth.

After the hour of psalm singing, I walked down to the pottery shop to pick out some earthenware pottery to take home. A water jug caught my attention. I liked its simple shape, the rings of clay. It felt cool in my hands. One of the sisters wrapped it in a sheet of newspaper. She walked with me back to the wooden gate at the entrance of the monastery and wished me well as I started my way down the mountain.

Not far from the top, I stopped to pick some wild flowers, which grow at high altitudes. I took only a few, in different shades of pink, to put in my water jug when I was back home. I wanted to bring some of the mountain down into the valley.

Further down, as the road hugs the steep side of the mountain, I heard the buzz of a bee in the back of the car. I continued to drive, hoping it would stay near the flowers. The incessant buzzing grew louder. The bee circled my head. I could not stop in the middle of the narrow road. It lunged through the middle of the steering wheel to settle on the dashboard.

I watched what it would do next. Then I looked up and saw the stone ledge coming straight at the car. It was too late to steer away. I drove straight into the ledge. The windows shattered. I held on to the wheel. The car heaved, rose up on its side and rolled over. The road, the mountainside, the blue sky went black. When I regained consciousness, I was still sitting behind the wheel. The car was right side up but on the other side of the road, facing the opposite direction and overlooking the fields far below.

I struggled to get out. My door had buckled under the squashed roof I pushed it open and squeezed through the smashed door. I looked for a place where I could lie down. As I crossed the road, I stumbled over the water jug. I picked it up, still wrapped in the one sheet of newspaper. I walked past the ledge and lay down on the hillside.

Cars stopped. I saw faces above me. Soon a siren sounded in the distance. I wanted to stand up but several hands held me firmly to the ground. The siren came closer and stopped. Ambulance drivers lifted me onto a stretcher. I was still holding the water jug. Someone handed me my purse. I looked back at my little yellow car. The front wheels had disappeared; it was on its knees.

The siren wailed all the way down the mountain to the hospital in Geneva. I was wheeled through dark corridors into a bright room where nurses and doctors examined me and took x-rays. Finally I was allowed to sit in a wheelchair and to answer questions. A nurse handed me my purse and the jug. A doctor came and said that he had found nothing broken, but he thought it best to keep me overnight.

I did not want to be alone that night. I signed a paper to be released and telephoned Pierre. He came quickly and drove me home.

On the way to the house, I unwrapped the water jug. It felt comforting to my hands. The jug was unbroken, without a scratch. Unmarred, smooth, and intact, as if it had never somersaulted across the road.

When we arrived home, I put it on the round wooden table in the kitchen. The water jug was safe.

ॐ

My Dutch friend was caught up in my story. She did not know about the accident.

"And you, you were really unbroken?" she asked.

"I was unbroken." I liked the way she used English words.

"Unbroken like the water jug," she said.

"Yes, but the story is not finished. Look at the jug. Turn it around. There, close to the bottom."

She held up the jug, looking near the bottom where I was pointing.

"See the slight crack, like a vein becoming visible with age? A few years ago the jug was unmarked. Then one day, not too long ago, I noticed that there was a very fine line, etching itself on the surface of the jug, working its way upward."

She ran her finger over the vein. The surface of the jug was smooth but the fine line was easy to follow.

"There wasn't any line at all?" she asked.

"No, there wasn't any line."

"And the jug hasn't fallen since?"

"No, it hasn't fallen since."

She carefully put the jug back in the middle of the table and looked at me. "Then what happened?"

I paused. "I think the crack is inside the jug. It's vulnerable like we are."

The Crack

In the monastery on top of mont voirons, the little sister turned the earthenware jug, one ring at a time. She turned the jug in silence. Her hands shaped the long spiral of dark gray clay from large circles at the bottom into smaller circles at the top. Slowly she smoothed the still moist surface, cupping her hands in prayer around the jug.

Only later, many years later, did the crack appear, climbing upward through the rings of clay. Like a fine vein it etched itself into the smooth surface, coming from deep within, from the silence of its creator.

FRANCE
1976 – 1983

Samoëns in Winter

La Bête Noire

FOR MANY YEARS WE WOULD LEAVE OUR RATHER SMALL house in Geneva to spend the weekend in the large family chalet in the mountains at Samoëns. It was something very French—and very Swiss—to go to the chalet in the mountains, especially in the wintertime when there was lots of snow and when the ski trails were beckoning.

Come Friday evening, I'd have the car packed and ready, so we could leave the city as soon as the working father arrived from his office. "There's less traffic after seven p.m.," Pierre would tell us, looking for an excuse for his long hours at the office. "The ride's much easier."

We had the largest station wagon we could find, a Peugeot *familiale, grand format*. When we drove all together in the car, I would take Daniel up front with me. The three older children sat on the middle seat, and the two younger all the way back. At first, whenever we were driving any distance, we used to shift the children around, wanting to be fair and democratic— rather American, I thought—about our family habits. Then we decided it was essential to have a few strict habits, or perhaps rules, and we assigned the seats according to age. "Don't worry, everyone will get his chance," their father reassured them.

The two younger ones weren't so sure, but then they had our collie with them on the backseat. Junon—a queen goddess, the wife of Jupiter—was a rather big dog for a crowded station wagon, but she was a wonderful family pet and a good traveler. She knew that otherwise she'd be left home alone.

Each child took along a gym bag, a sturdy cloth bag that school children in Geneva used during the weekdays for gym clothes and that we used during weekends for toothbrushes, pajamas, and whatever. There were also six sleeping bags and a pair of sheets for Pierre and me. Blankets were kept on each bed at the chalet. Every weekend I would offer to take more sheets for anyone who wanted to make his own bed, but the children always opted for sleeping bags.

Then there was the carton of food. "It's much easier to arrive with everything ready," Pierre said. And of course, it was no trouble to prepare and pack and take care of the children while the father was busy tidying up his desk at the office downtown.

I'd try to make it all fun. After all it was the thing to do, to go to the mountains for the weekend. The food went behind the last seat of the car because the skis went on the top, all sixteen of them. Ski boots went close to everyone's feet, except the driver's. He needed lots of room. I took his boots at my feet, along with my boots and Daniel's. I had learned long ago that there was always room.

We sang songs as we drove along. The chalet was only an hour away but an hour's ride could become long and tedious with eight of us in the same car and with less discipline than Pierre claimed to remember from growing up in his still larger family of ten children. So I led the songs, sometimes in English, sometimes in French, trying to keep everyone happy while Pierre drove. We'd sing *"Frère Jacques"* and *"Alouette, Gentille Alouette."* We'd sing "My Bonny Lies over the Ocean," and we would sway back and forth, from one side of the car to the other, always very careful not to hit the driver.

As we got closer to the chalet, we would start singing louder and louder, giddy and excited. Even the father would finally join in. *"Savez-vous planter des choux?"* We made up the verses. *"Savez-vous faire la fondue?"* That was for Saturday night, cheese fondue, every Saturday night during the entire winter. It was the father's specialty. The children and I would grate the cheese, cut the bread and set the table. Pierre would stand by the stove and stir the wine.

When we at last arrived, we'd rush out of the car to run around the chalet and roll in the snow with Junon. If there were fresh snow, we'd have to either shovel out the driveway in the dark or carry everything from the road across the yard to the chalet, including the sixteen skis and the sixteen boots and so forth.

While the father and three older children figured this out, I'd go inside with the three younger ones. Sleeping bags and gym bags went upstairs on each bed. The carton of food went into the kitchen, the boots on the steps to the cellar, and a fire in the fireplace. The house would be freezing when we arrived on Friday evening but it would warm up nicely by the time we left on Sunday afternoon.

We'd continue to jump up and down, hop and skip, and the youngest children would stand as close to the fire as they dared without getting burned. They were like pieces of toast in an old-fashioned toaster that needed to be turned every so often. I'd put water on to boil for pasta and warm my hands over the pot. I would have made the tomato sauce back in Geneva and brought it along in the carton of foodstuffs. It was easier this way, my husband had said.

When the older children came inside, they'd set the table, using as few plates and as little silverware as possible. They would not want to spend the evening washing dishes, especially washing dishes with cold water since the hot water, like the heat in the radiators, never got up to the faucets until Sunday. Instead they would want to clean up the kitchen quickly in order to play outside in the dark. In order to play *La Bête Noire*, The Black Beast, our favorite family game.

Even in the coldest and darkest of nights we would play. That only made the game more fun. After supper, and after the dishes, we'd choose straws to see who would be *la bête noire* – who would hide first and be the black beast while the rest of us tracked him down. Whoever drew the shortest straw would dress in a dark coat, with a dark woolen hat and dark woolen mittens, and then go outside alone to hide somewhere in the yard – behind the bushes, under the pine branches, alongside the back wall, on top of the wood pile. Junon would run along for company. They'd find their hiding place and together sit very still.

The rest of us would count to a hundred and then pile on coats, hats, mittens and scarves. We'd turn out all the lights in the chalet so that the yard would be inky black and so that even if we squinted real hard we wouldn't be able to see. When we were quite certain that *la bête noire* was well hidden, we'd follow one another outside and down the steps to the yard, holding on to someone's hand in order not to trip or stumble in the dark.

We'd stomp and shout and make all the noise we hadn't been able to make during the week back in Geneva. We'd also stomp and shout because we were just a little bit afraid to be outside in the dark, shooting for the black beast. But we'd never admit it, not even to ourselves.

As soon as one of us found him, very quietly, without letting anyone else see us, we'd slip in alongside him, hiding ourselves as best we could. Sometimes Junon's tail would give us away. We'd try to hold it still. And we'd try not to say *"chut!"*, not to giggle, not to make any noise. We would clamp our woolen mittens tight over our mouths, and then we would wait and watch as everyone else continued to hunt all around.

"Where are you?" they'd shout. *"La bête noire*, where are you?" We'd not make a sound.

"Woof," they'd shout, trying to get a growl out of Junon. We'd hold her tight in our arms. "Woof, woof!" they'd shout again. And we'd tremble, afraid that she might woof back at them.

Soon only five or four would be stomping and shouting around the yard. Then still another one would find us and squeeze in.

"Woof," the others would try again, "Woof, woof!", and we'd hold our breaths.

There would be three left, then two. This would become scary. Our hearts would be pounding, and we'd never let just one young child stomp around for long. It was too terrifying to be out all alone in the black night. And still we would wait.

It seemed it was always the father who was the last one out, who stomped around the yard, ranting and raging alone in the darkest of nights. Then, of common accord, the rest of us, all snug together in our hiding place, would change the rules of the game.

The father became *la bête noire*. We would huddle still tighter together, waiting to pounce on him. And when he'd get very close to us, and still closer, so close that we could hear him breathing, we'd jump out from behind the bushes, from wherever we were hiding, all seven of us, screaming and shouting, "*la bête noire!*"

Over the years, I no longer remembered the right rules for the game. Who was the black beast? The one who hid first alone or the one who was the last to find us? I only remembered that each of those Friday evenings in Geneva, when we'd pack ourselves into the car for another winter weekend in the family chalet, I'd wait my turn to get even with ... *la bête noire.*

FONDUE SAVOYARDE
(for four)

—◦—

The quality of the cheese is important. A mixture of Gruyère (not Emmental or Swiss that has holes) and Comté cheeses is best. The measures are without the rind. Kirsch is a brandy made from cherries.

6 cups grated Gruyère cheese	*1½ cups dry white wine*
1 ounce kirsch	*freshly ground pepper and salt*
2 cloves garlic	*dash of nutmeg*

Rub the earthenware pot with garlic. Warm the wine until it starts to bubble. Add cheese and bring to boiling point, stirring constantly in the same direction until mixture is smooth and creamy. Add a dash of nutmeg, salt and pepper to taste. Keep the fondue just simmering over a little fire. Stir in kirsch at the table and serve with small chunks of crisp French bread. And special forks with long handles. *Bon appétit!*

☞ *Coup du milieu: When the fondue is half finished, to whet the appetites, serve small glasses of kirsch.*

☞ *For a Fondue Royale use Champagne or another sparkling dry white wine.*

The Hay Chalet

Red Geraniums

CHURCH BELLS WERE RINGING CLOSE BY IN THE VILLAGE of Samoëns, twelve strokes skipped across the slate roofs. The mountains were misty, fading into purple in the distance. The haze was a favorable sign meaning the weather would remain warm and sunny with blue skies.

Papa and Maman, my father-in-law and mother-in-law, were waiting. Their children and grandchildren were gathering for the family midday dinner, as we did each Sunday in summertime.

"Susie, come on," Pierre called to me.

"Go ahead, I'm coming." I looked out the windows, over the flower boxes filled with geraniums, down to the backyard, the swings, the red clay tennis court, and the little hay chalet, carried down from the mountains years ago, before I arrived in the family.

"The children have already gone," insisted Pierre.

"I know." Minutes earlier I'd watched them disappear down the path to their grandparents' chalet. They had grown up with Sunday dinners.

Pierre waited patiently. "Susie?"

Even after twenty years, I still wasn't used to the way he said my name. He drew out the vowels, saying something that sounded like *suu-zii*. Slowly I went down the steps. The sky was porcelain blue, almost cloudless. The copper beach trees, the giant snapdragons, the cut grass, everything was shining in the sunlight.

"Why don't we go for a picnic?" I suggested. "Just the two of us?"

"We can't, not today. You know that. The family is waiting for us." He turned as I caught up with him. "Whom do you want to sit next to this time?"

"You," I answered, thinking how nice it would be to sit together at Sunday dinner.

But at Sunday dinners Pierre, the oldest son, always sat at Maman's right, and Monique, the oldest daughter, always sat at Papa's right. The rest of us sat wherever we wished except next to our spouses.

All nine children—Monique, Pierre, and the seven younger brothers—were married. The second daughter, Christine, died the year I studied at Grenoble, the night I first met his parents.

The nine were married in order, every two years, the way they were born. Now they were having children in order, every two years. Papa and Maman had over thirty grandchildren.

Eventually the children would get married in order, and then they would have children in order.

ॐ

Red geraniums beckoned to us from the windowsills of the parents' chalet. The tables were set like multicolored flowerbeds on the green lawn under the trees. I wanted to sing a Sunday song, do a dance, clap my hands, but Pierre's family was not effusive. They approached one another. They did not hug one another.

"*Bonjour Papa.*" I curtsied slightly and kissed my father-in-law lightly on both cheeks.

He was dressed in knee-length knickers and a beige sweater with a matching golf hat, as if he were walking out of the 1920s. He stood as always with his feet pointed straight sideways. Lucie, our young ballerina daughter, would be forever grateful to her French grandfather for his nimble toes.

"*Bonjour Maman.*" I curtsied just a little and kissed again.

My mother-in-law asked if I'd slept well. At first when she asked me this, I thought she was being indiscreet. Then I learned that French people always ask one another if they slept well. That's the first thing they say to one another each morning. "*Bonjour, as-tu bien dormi?*" And each morning they seem sincerely concerned.

She soon excused herself to go see about Sunday dinner. I watched her walk up the slope toward the open doors of the living room, her chignon as white as the single cloud brushed across the middle of the blue sky.

Papa rang the dinner bell, an old large bell like the ones worn by the cows high up in the mountains in summertime. The family responded and slowly moved to take their place. Soft sunlight nudged through the branches of the trees, playing shadows on the tabletops.

"*Bonjour,* my prettiest sister-in-law," said Maurice, the older sister's husband, the one brother-in-law who didn't look like all the others.

I was surprised to see him. He and Monique weren't expected this Sunday. Maurice, more gallant than Pierre's brothers, was always telling each of his eight sisters-in-law that she was the prettiest. I didn't mind. Pierre and his seven younger brothers never looked at their sisters-in-law. They wore blinders like well-bred race horses.

The adults sat down at the long table with the hand-embroidered green and white tablecloth. The older grandchildren took their places at the large round table with a flowered cloth. The younger grandchildren, including our Daniel who had learned to sit quietly at Sunday dinners, settled down at two little tables with paper cloths. Today there were thirty-three of us.

Thierry, the youngest son of the family, carried in two bottles of iced champagne. He was our wine butler for the day. It was always the youngest brother present who filled this role. With age, all the brothers looked more and more alike and more and more like Pierre—tall and slender, lots of curly dark brown hair, high foreheads, dark eyes, some even had the same dimple on the left side.

"It's a special Sunday," said Papa, standing up and raising his glass.

There was an expectant hush.

"We have our new grandson with us for the first time. I raise my glass to the proud parents."

I looked over at the black baby carriage sitting under the white birch tree. The carriage had been in the family close to half a century, carrying close to forty babies. It had held Pierre, his sisters, and all his younger brothers, and then each of ours. Now it held a new baby, a quiet baby, lulled by the preceding generations.

"Let's also toast the proud grandparents," said Pierre, fulfilling his role as the oldest son and standing up, to the right of his mother and opposite his father.

"Hear ye, hear ye! *Le prince* has spoken." Maurice waved his champagne glass in front of my face. He knew how much I disliked the nickname—*le prince*—for my husband. It was not so much a nickname as a title, inherited like an old family heirloom and still more difficult to get rid of.

I pushed Maurice's hand away. "His name is Pierre," I said, repeating myself once again.

"But, Susie, he'll always be *le prince*," said Thierry, coming up behind me with another bottle of champagne. "Nothing can be done about it. He was born that way."

"What way?" I asked.

Maurice leaned back out of the way, visibly delighted with the scene he had provoked.

"The way every prince is born, first," replied Thierry. He refilled my glass. "He's always first and I'm always last. Even on the tennis court, he's first." Bubbles of champagne overflowed. "What can I do?" he asked. "He always wins!"

"It's true," said Colette, his young dark-haired wife.

Thierry frowned and moved farther down the table with his bottle of champagne.

"Colette," I said, "that can't be true."

"It is, but they haven't played for a long time. Maybe this afternoon they can play together."

I looked down the table. People had stopped talking and were listening. Pierre was staring at me. His eyes were suggesting that I talk about something else, something less personal, less intimate, something more appropriate for Sunday dinner.

♂♥

The older grandchildren were serving the adults, and the middle grandchildren were serving the younger grand-children. Summer after summer, year after year, they rehearsed their roles.

I looked at the red geraniums in the flower boxes on the windowsills all around the chalet. They were especially lovely this summer, bursting into bright crimson. My mother-in-law kept the same ones year after year, putting them in the cellar during the winter, then placing them back in the spring.

At the beginning of our marriage, I tried to do the same thing but the plants never blossomed properly the second year round. By the fourth year, they barely grew leaves. Then one spring I decided to leave them in the cellar and buy new ones. The following spring, I threw out the old ones and started buying new ones every spring.

It wasn't the only thing I tried to do to emulate my mother-in-law. She initiated me in the art of yogurt-making by giving me lots of bottles and brushes, pots and pans. I washed and rewashed the bottles—that's what the brushes were for—and the pots and the pans. It all smelled awful. Only our first two children got to taste my homemade yogurt. It was never very firm or very smooth. The other children enjoyed store-bought yogurt, both firm and smooth, with different flavors and colors.

"Françoise, do you make your own yogurt?" I asked, trying to find a more neutral subject of table conversation and addressing my innocent question to the sister-in-law with whom I was the closest, both in age and affinity.

"No, I don't really like yogurt," she answered,

"What a pity!" said Maurice. "There's nothing quite like homemade yogurt."

"Well, I make yogurt for Thierry," said Colette.

"Do you really?" I asked. I pictured myself twenty years back, with pots of smelly yogurt germinating around the entire kitchen.

"Yes," assured Colette. "Thierry really likes it."

Pierre was looking at me again. Even yogurt was too intimate for Sunday dinner. The conversation paused.

People sipped their champagne. I decided that perhaps I should talk about the red geraniums and tell my mother-in-law how lovely they were, especially this summer.

Just then Monique, the oldest sister, asked for the family's attention. Maurice stopped staring at his sisters-in-law and sat up straight. Everyone listened. Monique took a deep breath and announced the forthcoming marriage of their second son.

There was startled silence.

The son in question was not there, nor was his older brother. No one was expecting a wedding announcement. It had been several years since the last of the marriages. The whole family was out of practice. Besides, Papa and Maman were waiting for Monique's first son, their oldest grandson, to get married. Now, instead, number two was stepping out of place and getting married first.

No one spoke.

A second cloud appeared in the blue sky, the trees whispered, the tablecloths rustled. Monique was waiting for her parents' approval. Even the grandchildren were standing still with their silver serving trays, so many statues in the sunlight.

"Here's to the future newlyweds," I said, standing and raising my glass. "And here's to their parents and to their grandparents."

The family stirred. The ripple passed. Thierry went back for more champagne. Corks popped like fireworks. Papa and Maman congratulated Monique, their one daughter. Maurice sank back in his chair with relief. Conversation zigzagged down the long table under the trees.

Pierre was smiling at me. Red geraniums, tennis matches, homemade yogurt, Sunday dinners. Another summer, maybe not too far away, it would be one of our children getting married, in or out of order. And the family would celebrate with champagne.

Maurice alone was quiet. I turned to see if he'd fallen asleep in the midst of the excitement.

"Maurice, are you sleeping?" I asked, poking him gently.

"No, I'm recovering."

"Maurice, did you and Monique come especially to announce the wedding?"

"Yes," he answered. "It was Monique's idea. Thirty years ago, almost to the very day, we announced our own engagement right here at Sunday dinner."

I thought back. That was before I had come to France. Before I had ever thought of coming to France. "And were there red geraniums then?"

"Susie, there were always red geraniums."

The mountains remained misty and the sun grew warmer. Our thirteen-year-old daughter, Lucie, arrived arm-in-arm with her favorite cousin, Nicolas, carrying together the large tray of vanilla and chocolate ice-cream cups for the younger grandchildren. The two cousins were the same age and looked surprisingly alike.

"Lucie, stand up straight," scolded Maman, gently but firmly. "Nicolas, hold the tray with both hands, shoulders back!"

Lucie took back her arm and stood up straight. Nicolas lost hold of the tray, and the ice-cream cups went rolling over the grass and under the tables. The younger grandchildren went tumbling after them, all too happy to roll on the ground. Lucie and Nicolas burst into waves of laughter.

Maman couldn't keep a stern face. She let the little ones leave the table, taking their ice creams with them and going to play on the swings near the tennis court.

Lucie went back inside to fetch the second dessert tray with the traditional blueberry sorbet, made from the little berries which grew wild on the side of the mountains and which is prepared in the local pastry shop. The sorbet was cool and refreshing and gave us all purple-colored lips.

Coffee was served with chocolates. The leaves fluttered lazily in the light breeze. The older grandchildren came to say thank you to Maman and Papa and to ask to be excused.

Lucie and Nicolas walked in single file and then rushed off with the other cousins to warm up the court for the match between Uncle Pierre and Uncle Thierry.

We finished our coffee and sat quietly, enjoying the warm sun on our backs.

"Susie," said Françoise, "when is your next trip to America?" The question floated above the empty cups.

I looked around for an answer. "I don't know, maybe next summer. Right now it seems..." I was quiet as I looked for my words.

"It seems?" she repeated.

"It seems very far away. Like there's here and there's there, and I'm somewhere in the middle."

A red and white hang glider swooped down the mountainside and stayed suspended in the blue sky directly above our heads.

Next to me Maurice was napping. He had not heard my lofty statement.

ॐ

Papa and Maman stood up. The dinner had ended. The sisters-in-law started to collect the cups and saucers.

Pierre came and gave me a kiss on the forehead. "Thanks for your toast, for what you said. We'll have our picnic tomorrow," he said. "I promise you, just the two of us with the children." He looked at me, wanting me to smile. "And now, will you come and watch us play?"

"I'll come. I think the whole family will come and watch." I stood up and stretched in the afternoon sun. "Maybe just this time," I said softly, "you could let Thierry win."

"No secrets," said Maurice, who alone was still sitting in his chair. "Not at Sunday dinner."

Pierre nodded. His brothers were waiting for him. I watched them go off together to the tennis court. Pierre was the tallest. I wondered what Thierry would do about that. But first the tennis match.

I put my coffee cup and saucer on the tray and carried it to the chalet. Everything had been cleared away. Françoise and I folded the green and white tablecloth and went to thank Papa and Maman. They were standing by the baby carriage under the birch tree, admiring their youngest grandson. Papa's hand was resting on Maman's shoulder.

"Thank you for Sunday dinner," said Françoise.

"It is our pleasure," replied Papa.

"And the red geraniums," I added, "are especially lovely this summer."

Maman smiled. "Yes, they grow more lovely from one summer to the next."

Red Geraniums, Samoëns

In the Light

WE FINISHED PACKING THE STATION WAGON. ONLY THE wet bathing suits were still hanging on the line off the back porch. We had taken our early morning dip in the lake. It was time to head home.

I asked my husband to take a picture. We settled ourselves on the bluff, overlooking the water. I was in the middle, the children on both sides, some sitting, some standing. I wanted the photo close up, with all the faces in the light.

Our youngest was too close. He wouldn't be seen. Someone said to back up. He lost his balance and started to fall. I caught his hand and held tight. Pierre snapped the photo.

The Old House, Prévessin

The Old House

EVER SINCE I FIRST MOVED TO EUROPE, I DREAMED ABOUT living in a beautiful old house in the countryside, like the ones in the *House and Garden* magazines. So when our house in Geneva grew too small for us, I started looking for something larger and older, further out in the country, and on the other side of the border, in France, near the lycée where the children were going at Ferney-Voltaire.

I found an ancient priory—with ivy-covered walls, wooden lintels over the windows, a stone archway at the entrance, an old fountain and a winepress in the courtyard. Monks had lived there for centuries. Upstairs, in the master bedroom, once perhaps the chapter meeting room, there was an oak beam, carved deep with the date 1565.

Not far away on the hillside, an old chapel dated back to the same period. It was said that the monks had dug a tunnel from the priory to the chapel so that they could go back and forth freely, unmolested by thieves and nonbelievers. Our children turned over part of the backyard, hunting for the passageway.

They found some pewter spoons and bits of broken pottery, but no trace of a tunnel.

At the turn of the century when the last monks died and no new ones arrived to take their place, the house was abandoned and fell into a period of neglect. Finally a doctor from Paris bought it. He repaired the slate roof, the broken windows and shutters, and made certain all the doors locked. The entrance was redone, with a new gate, and the yard replanted—pink rhododendron close to the stone wall in the shade, rose bushes in the sunny corners, and rosemary and thyme near the kitchen door.

The family was never able to enjoy the old house. The doctor died of a heart attack very soon after they moved in. His wife didn't survive the death of her husband, and their only child, a daughter, moved back to Paris. She put the house up for rent and kept in touch with the closest neighbor, a meddlesome farmer who lived next door, and whose dilapidated cow barn was just across the road from our front door.

The old house was still partly furnished. We were instructed to put whatever we didn't need up in the attic that ran the entire length of the house. There was a trapdoor with a folding ladder. The space was immense and filled with antique tables, armchairs, cupboards, and lamps. There were cartons of books and photographs. Most of the furnishings were carefully covered with layers of plastic. A round walnut table with silver candlesticks reigned in the middle. Some of the Louis XV armchairs were uncovered, a faded blue silk scarf was lying on one of them.

ès

The children loved the old house. For the first time each one had a room of his own, like the monks centuries earlier. There were doors and corridors everywhere, creaking floors and secret crannies in the walls, calling out to play hide and seek. We put the Ping-Pong table in what was once the wine cellar, one step down from the kitchen. It opened into the courtyard where the winepress still stood in its broken splendor. Pierre cleaned out the old stone fountain and filled it with water. The children splashed in it when the sun got too hot. And in late summer petals from the climbing pink roses floated gracefully.

The farmer who lived down the road never looked with favor upon our arrival. When I'd say hello, he'd turn his head the other way and grunt something under his breath. His old felt hat was pulled so low it half hid his face. He always wore the same dark blue overalls and dirty boots, caked with cow dung. Every morning he would stalk about in front of our house, as if trying to get a glimpse of us, before disappearing into his dark barn.

The day of our housewarming, he gave us his own welcome. After our guests arrived and when the courtyard was filled with friends, a bellow burst forth from across the road. We rushed to the front yard, and there on the other side of the road, a brown and white spotted calf was hanging by her hind legs, head down, in the middle of the open barn door. Her neck was slit, and blood was gushing out into a wide basin below. Pierre tried to reassure our guests, saying it was like the father who killed the fattened calf to welcome home his prodigal son. But when we returned to the picnic table, groaning under pâtés and sausages, smoked hams and salamis, we had lost our appetites.

ঌ

As the months went by, strange things started to happen in the house. I had taken to leaving on a light at the top of the stairs when I went to bed. It reassured me when I woke in the middle of the night and when Pierre was traveling. The whole house so cracked and creaked with age that I often thought someone was walking up and down the long hall. I soon realized the light was burning out more often than normal. Sometimes I'd put in a new bulb, and the very next morning it would have burned out. When Pierre tried putting in the new light bulb, it stopped burning out, at least for a while. He told me that I must have been putting the bulb in the wrong way.

Then one night, when he was again traveling, I heard steps, short quick steps, above my head in the attic. I listened and they soon stopped. But when I tried to go back to sleep, *toc-toc, toc-toc*, the sounds came back. I got up and went into the hall. The folding ladder to the attic was in place. I asked myself if someone could pull it up from above. And if so, then could someone lower it from above? I stood there under the trapdoor not knowing what to do.

One of the bedroom doors opened. It was my oldest daughter. "Did you hear it too?" she asked. "It must be a pigeon caught in the attic." And there it came again, *toc-toc, toc-toc, toc-toc*. Of course, I thought, it was a pigeon. In the spring they had come and settled on a corner of the roof. One of them must have entered the attic and didn't know how to get back outside. I gave my daughter a hug, and we both went back to bed.

The next morning when the children had all left for school, I pulled down the ladder and went upstairs to the attic. Everything was as I remembered it. And there was no trace of a pigeon.

Another time it was a shutter swinging back and forth somewhere downstairs that woke me. I went down and checked all the windows. It was at the front window in the dining room, the window that looked out on the road. Pierre was again away. I tried to latch it from inside, but it was difficult and I had to go outside to do it. The almost full moon tinted the gray stones of the house silver. I closed the shutter tight and quickly went back inside.

From then on, I'd often hear the same shutter swing open in the middle of the night, even when I had fastened it tight before going to bed. I'd go downstairs and close it again. Sometimes I'd just turn over and go back to sleep. If Pierre were traveling, I'd tell him about it when he came back. He'd tell me it must have been the wind, but I didn't remember any wind.

The years passed, and we grew accustomed to the ways of the old house. From time to time the light at the top of the steps burned out, footsteps scurried across the attic floor, or the front shutter swung open and then clattered back and forth. We no longer paid any attention. We felt at home in our old house.

Often when we had company, we'd tell them stories about the monks, and sometimes we'd give guided tours of the entire house, right up through the trapdoor into the attic. It was after such an evening as I was cleaning up downstairs that I found a blue silk scarf on one of the Louis XV armchairs in the living room. The armchairs belonged to the house. The next day I telephoned our friends who had been with us, but no one had left behind a scarf.

Then I remembered having seen a similar scarf upstairs in the attic when we first moved in. Were there now two blue scarves? I pulled down the folding ladder and went up to look. The scarf was nowhere to be seen.

Shortly afterwards our next-door farmer stopped my husband as he was coming out of the driveway. He said that he was surprised we were still in the house. We were the first tenants to stay more than one year. The others had come and gone in rapid succession. And each time they moved out, they spoke about strange happenings in the house.

Pierre said that the farmer pushed back his hat and screwed up his eyes, expecting him to say something. But as Pierre didn't reply, the farmer continued, saying that the wife of the doctor had never gotten used to living alone in the house. It seemed she lost her mind and kept thinking the doctor would come back. Every evening she would wait for him, setting the dining-room table with silver candlesticks. Weeks and months went by, and each night she expected her husband to come home for dinner.

The farmer said she used to watch for him from the front window of the dining room. That's how each evening he saw the table set and the candles burning. Then one night the shutter stayed closed, all the next day it stayed closed, and still the next.

They had to break into the house. The wife had hanged herself, in her bedroom, above her bed. There was a very old beam there, the farmer said, with a date on it. It was from that beam that she hanged herself. They had to use a ladder to pull her down.

Pierre said he wasn't interested in any of it. He said he and his family were happy in the house, and he didn't want to worry about the doctor's wife. I would have liked to agree with him and put it all out of my mind. But instead, every night as I lay in bed, I'd look up at the oak beam and I'd imagine the doctor's wife hanging from it, just above our bed. I'd wonder how she'd gotten herself up there. Where was the ladder? And what had she used around her neck? A rope, a belt, or something softer?

I would watch to see if the light in the hall went out. And I'd wait to hear the steps, the quick little steps, scooting back and forth in the attic. Was she perhaps setting the table, the big walnut table in the middle of the attic? But then why did the front shutter bang back and forth downstairs in the dining room? There was no wind, not even the slightest breeze.

Not too long afterwards I said to Pierre that I thought it was time to move back to our house in Geneva. He thought so too and said he was tired of crossing the border each day to go to work. Our three oldest children were now going to university and were coming home only during vacations. Our three younger children were ready to share rooms again. Finally we were all ready to leave the old house—the creaking floors, the footsteps in the attic, the swinging shutter, and above all the meddlesome farmer next door.

Only when we were safely settled, back in our smaller house, did I tell the children the story about the doctor's wife who had lost her mind after her husband died. I told them the story as the farmer told it to Pierre. And often when it was late at night, I would tell the story anew.

I'd imagine the doctor and his wife sitting down to dinner. The walnut table would be set in the dining room. There'd be a white tablecloth and candlelight. And the woman would be wearing a blue silk scarf, tied—oh so loosely—around her neck.

The Statue of Voltaire, Ferney

Graffiti at the Lycée

OUR YEARS AT THE LYCÉE IN FERNEY-VOLTAIRE WERE unique. Monsieur le Proviseur was the first French school director I knew. He was short and often stood on his toes. His wife was British, an actress. She found Ferney-Voltaire provincial and longed to be in London.

I was new to French lycées, and new to French associations of parents. When I went to my first parents' assembly, I was expecting something like a Parent Teacher Association meeting in the States, instead it was more like a parents' soccer match— boisterous, if not down-right belligerent.

A large group of angry parents crowded together in one corner of the auditorium. When the Proviseur took the microphone to announce that once again the national education budget had been cut, they singled out the culprit, naming the current Prime Minister and started chanting, "*A-bas-Pom-pi-dou, A-bas-Pom-pi-dou.*"

The lycée was in its early years, and there were not enough teachers or classrooms for everyone. I learned that both professors and classrooms came from Paris and that Ferney-Voltaire was twice removed—once by distance, five hundred kilometers, and twice by the Jura Mountains. People in Paris didn't know where Ferney-Voltaire was. They even suspected that it might be Swiss.

Our oldest son, Peter, was in the first class to go straight through the seven years of lycée to the national *baccalauréat* exam. He was also in the class that from the start had the fewest professors. One year he went without math, another year without history.

In protest I joined the Parents' Committee. We cornered and pressured the Proviseur to no avail. We wrote letters to the next administrator in line, the Inspector in Bourg, then to the Rector in Lyon, and finally to the Minister in Paris. We respectfully requested, we cajoled, we threatened.

It took close to seven years of controversy, demonstrations, and strikes. When Peter and other students marched through the streets, the Parents Committee held a sit-in with the Proviseur, trying to force the hand of the Minister of Education in Paris. And when the Proviseur sided with the Minister, we took to the streets with the students. We circled the statue of Voltaire in the center of town, stopping all traffic.

Not only was the lycée trying to get established, it was simultaneously struggling to become international. Besides looking for French teachers, the administration was also looking for national teachers from the countries represented in the new program. As more national professors arrived, the lycée needed still more classrooms.

Again the Parents Committee wrote to the Inspector, wrote to the Rector, wrote to the Minister. We threatened more sit-ins, more strikes, with or without the students. Finally trucks arrived from Paris, over the Jura Mountains, carrying prefabricated classrooms.

Now Ferney-Voltaire is a marshy region. It was swampland until Voltaire drained the green hills that overlooked Geneva. The clay drain pipes, more than two hundred years old, still lie buried in the ground. This practical side of Voltaire's genius is ignored. As are the marshes of Ferney. So the prefabs were plopped down with no thought to proper drainage. Soon the teachers were complaining about frogs croaking underneath their new classrooms.

Meanwhile the lycée was officially declared international. The Minister congratulated the Proviseur and promised him at last a transfer to London.

There would be a fair to celebrate, the first international school fair. It would be held in June when the first class of students—Peter's class—was graduating. Invitations were sent to parents, to the Mayor, the Inspector, the Rector, the Minister. The buildings were cleaned and scrubbed. Displays and exhibits were prepared. Spirits were high.

But the day before the fair, dozens of pink flowers blossomed overnight on the front wall of the lycée. The Proviseur decided to call off the fair. The Parents Committee besieged his office. We arrived with three professional painters and while we wrangled with the Proviseur, the painters repainted the façade.

The fair was salvaged. One could barely see where the flowers had once bloomed.

It was a grand fair. Monsieur le Proviseur greeted everyone. He did not stand on his toes. He appeared to have grown taller. Monsieur le Ministre and Monsieur le Recteur had excused themselves. Monsieur l'Inspecteur was expected but he did not get across the Jura Mountains. Monsieur le Maire was present and requested that the students henceforth be kept from demonstrating on the streets.

With a certain fanfare, music even and a rolling of drums, the lycée was officially named the International Lycée of Ferney-Voltaire.

The next day I found a bucket in our garage. There was some paint at the bottom of it, a bright pink, the same color as the flowers that had blossomed on the front of the lycée. Peter and his friends had all passed their baccalauréat exams and were going on to university. Peter was going on to medical school. After seven years, he was leaving the lycée to his brothers and sisters.

I carefully washed away the trace.

Ode to the Potato

PIERRE AND I DO NOT PERCEIVE THE POTATO THE SAME way. Many years ago, when we visited the Krüller-Müller Museum in Holland and looked at van Gogh's *The Potato Eaters*, I realized that the potato was proof of our different cultures. Pierre stared at the dark painting as intensely as if he were looking at *The Last Supper*. I skipped over it, thinking how strange such a solemn gathering around a simple platter of potatoes.

Coming from two cultures and two sides of the ocean, we have tried—over close to thirty years of marriage—to bridge our differences. To find a way to keep a balance between his tastes and habits and my tastes and habits. And often it has been the smallest things, things that seem the least worrisome, like the potato, which have remained the peskiest.

When I grew up in a family of four in New York, we ate at the most twenty potatoes a week. And we never served them every day. When Pierre grew up in a family of twelve in northern France, they ate four hundred and twenty each week.

And they served them not only every day, but they served them twice every day.

During the first years of our marriage, when we were living in southern France, I found his fancy for potatoes simple and quaint. I would cheerfully peel four or five potatoes every day, but only once. Boiled, scalloped, mashed, or browned, I complied.

When we moved to Brussels, I even French-fried them as did my Belgian neighbors. I would peel and cut the potatoes lengthwise, all the same size, and then I would cook them in a deep fryer to make them crisp. Pierre said they were still better than the ones he remembered from his childhood in northern France.

But by the time we moved to Italy with three young children, I was beginning to feel the fatigue of peeling twenty potatoes every day. I suggested that when in Italy we should do as the Italians do and eat pasta instead. All that was needed was a big pot of boiling water.

Then our fourth child was born and for Mother's Day Pierre handed me a large and heavy gift-wrapped box. He was elated. I unwrapped it. It was an electric potato peeler. He said he remembered how easy it was at his parents' house where a potato peeler was permanently installed below the kitchen sink. When I first arrived in his home, I thought it was a garbage disposal, and from time to time I stuck orange peels down it. After a short period of time, my mother-in-law informed me it was not a garbage pail but a potato peeler and proceeded to show me how it worked.

Her machine could take a dozen small potatoes at a time, and in three minutes it supposedly peeled them. It would spin, the potatoes would swirl against the abrasive sides of the large round peeler while running water would wash off the dirty peels. When the machine was turned off and the trap door opened at the bottom, out tumbled twelve spotted potatoes. Each one would then have to be cleaned by hand, with a paring knife to get rid of the spots and the eyes. And if ever the three minutes lasted too long, the potatoes would keep swirling until they washed away, including the spots and the eyes.

In Italy, Pierre found a smaller version of the electric peeler. It did not attach below the kitchen sink, but instead stood on the counter or the kitchen table. It could take up to six medium-sized potatoes and just enough water to cover them. When it was turned on, the machine would start to jump up and down, spouting water everywhere. After three minutes, the six potatoes looked about the same as in the beginning, but not the tabletop or the floor.

I thanked Pierre and used it regularly, reminding myself that it was the intention that counted. But when we moved to the States for one year, with now five young children, I hinted that there might not be room for the electric potato peeler. In fact I decided to leave it with my Italian neighbors as a lasting souvenir of their French and American neighbors.

Once in the States, I put down my foot and said that was enough, no more potatoes for a year. I told Pierre that Americans no longer grew them, that they were too expensive, that I had no place to store them. And every now and then, when he kept asking for a *pot au feu*—with chunks of beef, onions, carrots, leeks, and lots of potatoes—I would buy little white peeled ones in tin cans. They were slippery and tasteless. But I was finally saying no to potatoes.

Then we moved to Switzerland, having realized that we manage our biculturalism better in a neutral country. For one year, Pierre had been blaming me for everything he didn't appreciate in the States, from the lack of French cheese to the apparent lack of fresh potatoes. And I could remember doing the same thing each summer in France, when we spent our vacations at his parents' chalet in the Alps, once the local color had worn off, including the novelty of his mother's electric potato peeler.

Now in neutral Switzerland, I discovered frozen French fries. It was so very easy to fix them that we went back to eating potatoes, but only frozen French-fried ones. They were already peeled, cut, and prepared. All I had to do was put them in hot oil for a couple of minutes before serving. The children loved them. Pierre said they didn't have the same taste, nor were they as crisp as the unfrozen ones I made once upon a time back in Belgium. I nodded.

Our sixth child arrived, and for Mother's Day, Pierre gave me a second special gift. It wasn't as large as the first very special Mother's Day gift, and it seemed as light as air. It was probably wrapped up in pretty pink paper with a pink ribbon. I don't remember. I only remember the contents, a box of instant mashed potatoes.

After sixteen years of marriage and six children, my husband was giving me a box of potato flakes for Mother's Day. I wanted to throw the whole thing at him, the flakes and the box and the pretty pink paper. But the children were watching, eagerly waiting to taste their mother's instant mashed potatoes.

Soon afterwards, as I was happily alternating frozen French fries and instant Swiss mashed potatoes, our oldest son, Peter, introduced us to his first girlfriend. She was French, lived near the Jura Mountains, and went to the same lycée as our children did at Ferney-Voltaire. Her father was a farmer, a potato farmer. He harvested six hundred tons of potatoes every year.

We met her parents. We became friends. They had six children as we did. Our younger children played together. Their favorite playing place was the potato hangar where the six hundred tons of potatoes were stored at the end of each summer. There were mountains of them. If the father wasn't around, they would have potato fights, climbing to the top of the bumpy potato haystacks to take better aim.

When we went for dinner at their house, there would always be a piping hot platter of potatoes in the middle of the large table. Pierre would let himself be coaxed into refilling his plate at least twice. When he said he didn't eat fresh potatoes at home, our friends wouldn't believe him. Together they'd talk potatoes for a good part of the evening. Our farmer friend cultivated four different varieties. Pierre learned to recognize them by taste. Then when we drove home at the end of the evening, our hosts would invariably give us a ten-kilo bag of his current favorite variety.

ॐ

Some ten years later, Pierre and I found ourselves again almost alone in the house. Only our two youngest were still at home. So I went back to cooking a few fresh—unfrozen and unflaked—potatoes for my French husband. Maybe it was because he had finally learned to peel them with me. Or maybe it was because I had finally bought a second peeling knife.

GRATIN DAUPHINOIS

—◄o►—

To make this dish even more delicious, cut the potatoes paper-thin, and cook them until they are golden brown on the top but still moist underneath.
Pre-heat over to 400 F.

12 medium potatoes	*½ pound of butter*
2 cups of whole milk	*1 cup of cream*
Salt and freshly ground pepper	*nutmeg*

Spread the thin slices of peeled potatoes in shallow baking dish. Dot each layer with butter, salt and pepper, and cover with milk up to half of the layer. Do this twice. For the third layer, cover with cream just up to the layer. Sprinkle with nutmeg. Bake for 1 hour to 1 ½ hour, until top layer is browned and milk has been absorbed but potatoes are still moist.

90th Birthday Dinner, Tourcoing

The Chesterfields of Grandmére

PIERRE'S GRANDMOTHER WAS NINETY-NINE YEARS OLD
when she asked me to write her story. She carried a little
black notebook in her purse where she kept track of her
descendants—dates of births, baptisms, first communions,
marriages, also diplomas and professions.

It was when she started to look through the professions for a
storyteller that she turned to me and said, *"Alors, ma petite fille
américaine, c'est à toi."* "Well then my American granddaughter,
it's up to you!" And she told me to get on with it because she
wasn't going to be around forever.

I first met Grandmère thirty years earlier, after Pierre and I were
engaged. His parents drove us from their chalet in the French
Alps to the maternal family home in Tourcoing, in northern
France, where I was to be formally introduced to their relatives.
There would be over seventy of them at the reception. I wrote
down the names of the aunts and uncles and tried to learn as

many as I could on the way. With my small family in the States, I had no practice at this.

Grandmère was waiting for us. The high wrought-iron gates opened to formal rose gardens, circular lawns, flower beds, and carefully trimmed shrubs. "Welcome, *ma petite fille*," she said, taking my hand in both of hers. Dressed in light gray silk, with her silver white hair, she reminded me of a daguerreotype.

She spoke excellent English. She told me later that instead of letting her study mathematics with her brothers, her parents had sent her to Oxford to study English, "*beaucoup plus convenable pour une jeune fille*," "much more suitable for a young lady."

She led us into the large entrance hall, where Grandpère was waiting to meet us. He stood very tall and straight, formally attired, an elegant mustache, his hand on a black and silver cane. He had studied mathematics and science, as had Grandmère's brothers, before taking over the family textile business. He stood that day in the background. This is how I would always see him, standing tall and straight behind Grandmère.

The hall was lined with antique tapestries. There was a crystal chandelier in the center of the room, a wide staircase at the far end, and beautiful pink gladioli on the grand piano. I learned that during World War II, when German officers sequestered the house and Grandpère and Grandmère fled to the south, the piano had been splintered and the finest of all the tapestries had disappeared. A few years after the war, Grandmère found the missing tapestry in the cellar, rolled into a dark corner.

The German officers built a bunker right in the middle of the rose garden. The walls were so thick it was impossible to demolish them without blowing up the entire house. The bunker still stands there. Each year the gardener plants more rose bushes, training the branches to climb over the bunker and the red roses to conceal the harsh souvenir of the war.

The day after our arrival the two reception rooms were filled with bouquets of cut flowers—more pink gladioli, yellow lilies, fuchsia snapdragons. Grandmère told me where to stand. Pierre was at my right to introduce his relatives. She was at my left to keep the line moving. She said I shouldn't worry about remembering names. I should look pretty and smile. People just wanted to see for themselves the young American who had won the heart of her grandson.

After the introductions, waiters circulated with glasses of champagne. Grandmère went to one of the cupboards and took out a carton of Chesterfields. There seemed to be an aura of secrecy about them. Where did they come from? Pierre could not tell me. He said they were a traditional part of each reception.

"*Seulement pour les grandes occasions*, only for special occasions," Grandmère said, as she opened a few packs and put the cigarettes on a silver tray. She apologized for the yellowish aging cellophane and said she hoped their aroma was still the same.

We were to be married during the following year in the States. Grandmère asked us to bring back a wedding portrait like the ones in gilded frames on the wall of their drawing room. Each bride was sitting on a Louis XV armchair, her long satin train spread out around her. The groom was standing to the side, stiff and self-conscious. There were five wedding portraits on the top row for her five married children. The lower rows were filled with similar formal wedding portraits of her oldest grandchildren. Grandmère's sixth child was a priest. His portrait, showing him dressed in a long black cassock, hung on another wall all alone.

When we sailed back to France, we brought her our wedding photo, less formal, with no Louis XV chair, no long train. We also brought a linen tea cloth for Grandmère and a bottle of New York wine for Grandpère. The wine was tasted and appreciated, as much as a bottle of American wine could be appreciated by a Frenchman. And the tea cloth stayed with a tiny white label sewn on the back, *"Pierre et Susie, à leur retour de l'Amérique, le 8 septembre, 1958."*

I learned to look more closely at the different objects around me in the house. For over half a century, Grandmère had marked each gift and souvenir with a name, a place, and a date. I picked up a crystal vase from Venice, marked with Pierre's parents' names on their tenth wedding anniversary. Grandmère took me upstairs to the attic where everything was neat and orderly and where every box, every carton had little white labels with names and dates.

Born in 1886, Grandmere's belongings spanned the century. She showed me the wardrobe trunk she had taken with her for her honeymoon on the Italian lakes. Each evening she would change her robe, and also her hat, gloves, shoes, and purse. Once it all fitted into the wardrobe trunk. Now each outfit was folded and wrapped in white tissue paper in flat boxes. She willingly lent them to her granddaughters and great granddaughters for formal evenings or costume balls, as long as everything came back, cleaned and carefully refolded in its flat box.

ॐ

The next time I saw Grandmère, we were living close by in Brussels. We would often spend the weekend at her house. The same Swiss governess who had taken care of her children now took care of our children. And Grandmère took care of me. Each morning I'd be served breakfast in bed and told to rest. Grandmère believed that young mothers needed to safeguard their strength. She told me she had stayed strong by sitting down whenever she didn't have to stand and by lying down whenever she didn't have to sit.

I never could imagine Grandmère lying down. Even when Pierre and I would come back late in the evening, she'd still be sitting in the drawing room with a knitted shawl over her shoulders and a rosary in her hands. *"Une prière pour chacun,"* she would say. "A prayer for each child, grandchild, and great-grandchild." If we caught her napping, her head nodding, she'd wake up and smile, telling us that the good Lord didn't mind.

During these visits, our children were on their best behavior. The decorum at mealtime awed them into silence. Our two oldest would spend the time counting the plates used during the four-course meals. Once five-year-old Peter managed to slide under the table just far enough to push the bell for the maid. Then he slipped back in place, pretending to have never budged. Grandmère let him get away with it and feigned surprise when the maid appeared. Little Peter was beside himself with glee. But when the maid returned to the kitchen, Grandmère turned to him, with a raised eyebrow, "*Seulement une fois, jeune homme!*" she said. "Only once, young man!" And Peter never tried again.

When Grandmère turned eighty, the entire family gathered together at her house to celebrate. We were living in Italy and arrived on the night train from Milano. Grandmère gave us rooms up on the top floor, where years earlier the maids had slept and where the Swiss governess still had her quarters. Our children were allowed the run of the entire house, up the back staircases and down the large front staircases, in and out of the kitchen and pantry. "*Laissez-les s'amuser*, let them have a good time," said Grandmère, "they're only children once."

At noon the next day a professional photographer arrived and managed to place all of us for the family photo. We were over one hundred descendants. We stood on the wide slope going down from the terrace. He told us when to smile.

Inside the tables glistened with silver and crystal. We toasted Grandmère's eightieth birthday. She said a few words. Her eyes filled with tears when she spoke of Grandpère. He listened and quietly smoked his pipe. It would be the last time many of us would see him.

After the dinner and the speeches, we moved into the drawing room for coffee. Once again Grandmère went to the cupboard where she kept her Chesterfields. She took out another full carton. As she opened it, she glanced at Grandpère who seemed to share her secret. How many more cartons were tucked away in the cupboard? And where had they been tucked away before they found their place in Grandmère's drawing room?

Ten years later, when Grandmère turned ninety, the entire family gathered yet another time. Grandpère had long since died. The governess had returned to Switzerland. One of the granddaughters had moved into the house to keep Grandmère company and help care for her. This time we stayed overnight at an uncle's house.

When the same professional photographer arrived and saw that we were over one hundred and fifty, he tried to excuse himself. Finally it was Grandmère who lined us up on the same wide slope near the terrace. When we were in place, she summoned back the photographer. All he had to do was push the button.

The tables were set on white damask table linen. After the *la mousse au chocolat*, a much appreciated tradition at Grandmère's anniversaries, a dusty bottle of cognac dating from 1876 was opened with great ceremony. It had aged a full century, ten years longer than Grandmère. The toasts were eloquent. Grandmère downed her glass. *"Pas mal du tout pour un siècle!*" she announced with approval. "Not bad at all for one century!"

Next came the Chesterfields. Grandmère had prepared them. Several packages were open on the silver tray. The cellophane has shriveled. This time there were also little individually wrapped chocolates on the tray. "These you may all enjoy," she announced. "They're better for your health."

Grandmère at ninety-one decided it was time to take her first plane ride. She wanted to spend time with her youngest daughter, Pierre's mother, in their chalet in the Alps. The flight passed without mishap, and from then on, Grandmère flew down each summer to spend a few happy weeks with her daughter and all of us at the chalet.

One summer when we were having tea, my father-in-law took it upon himself to tell Grandmère how many qualities she had bestowed upon her daughter. He said that his wife was so lovely and so exceptional that he had never once looked at another woman. Grandmère's blue eyes twinkled, "*Fainéant!*" she said. "Lazybones!"

It was several summers later that she asked me to write her story and told me to get on with it. She said she wasn't going to be with us forever. Before flying home, she wanted me to read it to her. I said I was waiting for her hundredth birthday in the spring to finish it. She listened quietly, nodding her head. She smiled about the Chesterfields, appreciating each innuendo but not willing to share her secret. Where did they come from?

Who had given them to her? Had there been an American officer? Grandmère smiled and shook her head.

Then in the fall, she forgot one morning to wake up. We went back for the funeral. Her son the priest celebrated the Mass in the same church where she had been baptized ninety-nine years earlier. Grandmère was laid to rest next to Grandpère in the family tomb.

In the spring, we returned to celebrate her hundredth birthday. Grandmère had planned the entire reception, the invitations, the menu, the wines. When coffee was served, the silver tray of cigarettes was ready. There was another little label in Grandmère's handwriting, "*les dernières Chesterfields, mai 1986.*" The last Chesterfields, May 1986. The secret lingers.

MOUSSE AU CHOCOLAT
(for six)

◄○►

To make this superb dessert, it takes very good semi-sweet dark chocolat, very fresh eggs, and a very strong arm to stir.

8 ounces of dark chocolate	*¾ cup of sugar*
3 T. of butter	*5 fresh eggs*
3 T. Grand Marnie	

Separate the eggs, beat the yolks in one bowl, and the whites (with a pinch of salt) in another bowl until stiff. Melt together in a large pot over a low flame the butter, chocolate, and sugar. Remove from the heat and add the Grand Marnier. Now add one large spoonful at a time, the yolks and then the whites, stirring constantly. Refrigerate for several hours before serving.

☞ *Delicious with or without a topping of whipped cream!*

SWITZERLAND
1984 – 1990

Our House, Geneva

Flashbacks

WHEN THE TELEPHONE RANG LATE THAT NIGHT, PIERRE rolled over on his side of the bed, and I reached to answer. Our children were spread out far from our home in Geneva. I once thought that when they started to spread out, I would start enjoying long nights of sleep, something which had eluded me ever since I started having babies. Maybe it was because I nursed our first baby, and then because I nursed all the following babies. Pierre couldn't nurse, so he slept.

I remembered a time when, in the middle of the night, I would go sit in the kitchen to nurse. I had a craving then for cold milk. I would eat bowls of cornflakes doused with cold milk. This would be supposedly the two a.m. feeding, but it could be any time during the night. We were living in Italy, and I was giving up on strict feeding schedules. When the baby cried, I nursed him. That was what everyone was doing in Italy.

Still earlier, when our first baby was born in southern France, it was when I wanted to do everything as well as my mother-in-law who had nursed ten babies. To help me along, she had given me a shiny chrome baby scale. I weighed my babies before and after each feeding to be sure they had taken their one hundred grams of milk. I must have spent entire months of my life weighing babies.

This baby scale was convertible. It could also be used as a kitchen scale. My mother-in-law showed me how to adapt it and said I could use it also for cooking, for weighing fruit and making jam and jelly. I didn't know much about weighing fruit. In the States, fruit came already weighed and packaged. I especially didn't know about weighing fruit in grams. I was still thinking in ounces. It was enough to weigh the baby in grams.

I nursed Peter, this first child, for eight months, getting up in the middle of each night to feed and weigh him. The scale glowed in the dark with phosphorescent readings. I learned to do it all—to first weigh him, then nurse him, and weigh him again—without turning on the light and therefore without waking Pierre. At eight months, when the baby had two upper teeth and two lower teeth, I weaned him directly to the cup, a silver baby cup engraved with his initials.

The second baby was born in Belgium. Pierre would sometimes brag about his American wife who had never given a baby bottle to his son. I began to think I'd found a new vocation, American wet nurse in Europe, and decided to go ahead and nurse the second baby for as long as I had nursed the first. But she got her teeth sooner so I stopped at seven months. Still no baby bottles to put on display. Only silver baby cups, each with initials. I placed the shiny chrome scale away in a cupboard. I wasn't into making jams and jellies, only into nursing babies.

Number three came while we were still living in Brussels. We belonged to a couples group from the church—six Belgian couples and us—studying the topic of love and marriage. All of the women were having babies and nursing them. We would bring them to the meetings at one of the homes. During the evening, five or six ripe breasts would be uncovered while we modestly nursed our babies. And while the men discreetly kept their eyes elsewhere.

It was after moving to Italy and with the fourth baby that I got my craving for cold milk and I grew lax on feeding schedules. I also grew lax on weighing schedules. Our number four was big and healthy. I told myself that a few grams more or less wouldn't really matter. Who would know? Even the Italian pediatrician seemed less concerned with the number of grams of each feeding.

We had found another couples' group with Italian and French couples, and the topic was now fecundity and children. Once again all of us were having babies. There were still more ripe breasts at our meetings. And the Italian husbands were less discreet or were the mothers less modest?

When we decided to have our fifth child, our friends were slowing down. Four children seemed like a good number to them. We were happy to welcome another. A month after Lucie's birth, we went to America for one year for Pierre's studies and research. We joined another couples group at the local church. This time I didn't try nursing at the meetings.

Even though I was convinced that American mothers made excellent wet nurses, I was also convinced that American mothers more willingly nursed in private at home.

I had packed the baby scale, thinking I would still use it from time to time, feeling it was part of me, part of all those years of having babies in Europe. But with the first visit to the pediatrician, I realized I now needed to convert the readings from grams to ounces. So I put the scale back in the trunk and started weighing Lucie in ounces and only at the doctor's office.

Number six came after we moved to Switzerland. Daniel was almost two when he arrived from Vietnam. He was already drinking from a cup, so still there were no baby bottles. I sort of regretted it, one or two baby bottles, to wash and polish and put on the shelf. There were no trophies to cherish and polish for breast-feeding. And the chrome scale was back in the closet waiting for grandchildren.

So, when the phone rang in the middle of that night, I reached for it—just as I used to get up and nurse, and Pierre used to sleep. I reached to answer and my husband rolled over on his side. I fumbled in the dark, looking for the receiver. What time of night was it? "*Allô?*" I said. And again, "Allô?" There was that second or two of silence, just long enough to let me imagine one hundred awful things which might be happening somewhere in the night to one of our children.

It might be our oldest son who lived in France, but I didn't think so. He never called much. He was the one for whom I had tried to do everything exactly right, the one I weighed before and after each feeding on the brand new baby scale. He was now married, and his wife was expecting their first baby at the end of the month. I had passed on the baby scale to them. They were both doctors and would know how to use it. Furthermore his wife was French. She would also know how to use it for weighing fruit for jelly and jam.

It was more likely number two, Cecile. She called more often than her older brother. She was still single and going to graduate school in the States. A few months ago she had telephoned at midnight—six in the evening her time—and said, "I was accepted..." I heard, "I was assaulted..." It was hard to decipher words across the ocean with my heart beating in my ears. "Please repeat that," I asked her. When it was she who called, I could tell almost instantly because of the echo. After the second of silence came an echo. My hello came back to me. This didn't used to happen, only since overseas communications started going by satellite instead of cable.

Our third child was working at a hotel in Rome. She remembered her Italian yet she went through moments of loneliness which made her want to call home. I tried to tell her that she should feel at home there. She used to live in Italy. Did she remember? She'd gone to kindergarten with lots of Italian children. She played with them in Italian. But she said it was different now, she'd grown up and moved away. She no longer had her family and friends around her. She was alone and living in Rome. And I should listen to her. "Mom, are you listening?" she would say.

Number four was in Lausanne, studying physics part of the time and playing piano the rest of the time. He was the one I decided would be fine even if I stopped nursing on a strict time schedule. He was like his older brother and never called much, not even from close-by Lausanne. In fact he called so seldom that when the phone rang and he said, "Hi, Mom, it's Chris," I was stricken with fright. "What's wrong?" I would ask. "Are you all right?"

Our fifth child was a dancer in Paris. She was only nineteen, and it was better not to think about why she might be calling. Sprained ankle, subway strike, student demonstrations, armed aggression. The last time the phone rang after midnight, it was she. There'd been a bomb scare in the subway and she'd been stranded for hours. Police had escorted her home. She was calling to tell me about it. She needed to tell someone so she called her mother. I didn't want it to be her on the phone, not again in the middle of the night.

Number six was on a school trip to Germany so this time it might also be Daniel. Daniel was the only one still living at home. He was fifteen. He wasn't too good at sleeping away from home. He missed his bed and his room. His brothers and sisters said we spoiled him—too much care, too much attention, our last child. They said we gave in too easily. Not enough discipline. There weren't enough brothers and sisters in his way.

Who was it? I held the phone close to my ear. The second or two of silence passed.

"*Allô?*" I repeated. There was no echo. It was not from overseas.

"Mom? It's Peter." It was our oldest son. His voice had a different volume, a new dimension. "You have a grandson. Mom, you're a grandmother."

I couldn't speak. My firstborn now had a child. A new generation, a grandchild. My sleeping husband turned over in the bed, opened his eyes, and smiled at me. He had been awake all along.

"Congratulations, grandmother," he said.

I held the phone in silence.

"Mom, are you there?" asked Peter. "You have your first grandchild."

I handed the phone to Pierre. Tears were spilling down my cheeks. Peter our first son was a father. My daughter-in-law was a mother.

I tried to tell my husband, the new grandfather, to give them my love and congratulations. To ask how was the new mother. Was she all right? And the baby? How much did the baby weigh? I remembered the scale.

"Tell them to forget the baby scale," I said. "Tell them to use it for making jam and jelly."

A Pebble on My Path

THIS PEBBLE IS GRAY AND ORDINARY, ONE OF MANY ON my path. I walk on it daily, crunching it into the ground. Nothing distinguishes it from the others. Until I pick it up and hold it in my hand.

When our six children sit around the dining room table, their features all look similar. When they talk together, their voices all sound similar. Until I listen to each one's story.

How many people live on the earth? Over six billion. Imagine a roll call. Quick, we must line up. A trumpet sounds. We take our place. Each one of us counts.

Our Front Door

Echoes

THIS MORNING I AM ALONE IN THE HOUSE, LISTENING TO the echoes of children. For close to twenty years, my life has been tuned to the Swiss school day. There has always been a child coming or going, a child home for lunch, a child home from class. Now for the first time the house is empty. I walk on tiptoe through the silent rooms.

I hear early echoes from when we arrived and tried to make room for everyone. The front door of solid oak opened and closed heavily as the children followed one another to school. I worked against the clock each morning getting ready for the long lunch break, eleven to one-thirty. Then I began to listen for the bicycles. Soon the heavy door swung back and forth, one thud after the other, until the children were all home.

The door stays shut this morning. No children will be pedaling home from school for lunch. I open the hall window to let in some sunshine. Shadows play on the wooden stairs. They keep me company.

I hear other early echoes from when we made room for number six from Vietnam. We turned the garage into a playroom and the wine cellar into a bedroom. We bought bunk beds and gave the small bedroom to our new son. The walls of his little room rang from nightmares of wartime.

ॐ

There were eight of us then, and some of the Swiss habits of discipline were helping. The children didn't shove and push. They didn't bump into one another. Even on the staircase, they stayed in line. If I listened carefully to the steps, the steps of each child, I could tell whose steps they were, which child was going up, coming down.

They took turns playing the piano. Six practice periods every day. Bach, Mozart, Schumann...Schumann, Mozart, Bach. I still know the pieces by heart. I can hum each one. The sounds came from the hall in the basement where we put the upright piano. There was an extra piano stool for playing duets.

Once four of our children played at the same recital at the Geneva Conservatory. A Swiss mother, sitting next to me, turned and asked why each child played the same instrument. Why not different ones? "It would be so lovely, a small ensemble," she said. It was hard to explain that they liked doing the same thing, one after the other. I remember instead telling her we had four pianos at home.

ॐ

I hear sounds of birthday parties: musical chairs, pin the tail on the donkey, potato races, all those games that the American mother organized six times each year for the Swiss schoolmates of her children. The whole house was turned topsy-turvy, with a donkey on the refrigerator door in the kitchen, chairs lined up in the hall, and potatoes rolled under the couch in the living room. We'd sing "Happy Birthday to you," or rather *"Bon Anniversaire à toi,"* that never quite sounded the same, even after years of practice.

There are echoes of holidays, Easter and the Easter Bell. The tradition comes from northern France where legend says that during Lent, the bells go to Rome to be blessed, flying home on Easter Sunday filled with gifts for all the children. The bell—an upside-down basket covered in tinfoil, with a bell and lots of little gifts attached—would slide back and forth on a rope from the balcony to the cherry tree. The bell would ring and the children would jump to catch whatever gifts they could before their father pulled the bell out of their hands.

Echoes of Thanksgiving, with the table set for family and friends. Often we invited neighbors and friends to share our feast and to listen to the story of the first harvest in the New World. One of our children would read the story out loud while we carried in the roasted turkey, creamed onions, fresh cranberry sauce, and all the traditional trimmings.

And joyful echoes of Christmas, when we decorated the tree in the middle of the front hall, and the children's excitement ran up and down the staircase. We whispered secrets as we decided upon gifts. And listened to Christmas carols, singing our favorite ones over and over until we heard imaginary sleigh bells in the snow outside the windows.

SUSAN M. TIBERGHIEN

Soon came the noise of the first mopeds in the driveway, of Beatles records giving way to rock music, of teenage voices filling the house. I remember the first "*boum*" or dance party, in the playroom down in the basement for our oldest son's fifteenth birthday. The boums gradually moved upstairs to the living room. The furniture was moved out, sometimes so were the parents.

The house was noisy during those years, the sounds collided. Doors banged shut. There were clashes and arguments— when to say no, when to say yes—curfews respected, curfews broken. Rooms cleaned, rooms not cleaned. Homework done, homework not done. Promises kept, promises broken. I wanted everyone to get along. "It will be all right," I kept saying, especially to myself.

Soon the children started to move on. After the oldest boy left for university, the voices in the house shifted. The next two were girls. The sounds were feminine. They drank tea in the kitchen and shared stories. There were slumber parties, mattresses on the floor. The telephone rang and rang. There were hushed conversations. Sometimes laughter, sometimes tears.

When the two older girls went to university, it was the turn of their younger brother, number four. He played jazz on the piano and brought in his musician friends with a set of drums and a bass fiddle. Late at night when we asked for quiet, they played poker on the Ping-Pong table in the basement. Sounds of dice even two flights down.

206

Then the sounds were muted as the youngest daughter studied in the morning and danced at the conservatory in the afternoons. I see her sitting at her desk in her room. I hear her calling to me, "Mom, do latitudes go up and down or do they go sideways?" I didn't remember. I looked it up in the encyclopedia and called back upstairs the answer.

Our piano-playing son went on to school in Lausanne and then to the States. Our dancer to school in Paris. Only our youngest remained at home. He moved into the bedroom in the basement. The sounds grew louder with "house music." He made loudspeakers. The wooden boxes stood more than three feet high. The crescendos bounced off the walls. The lights blinked on and off as the playroom became a disco. His friends arrived on souped-up mopeds, brakes screeched to a halt in front of the front door.

ॐ

This morning he went for his first day as an apprentice in radio and hi-fi. The house is empty. I tiptoe from room to room, picking up forgotten books, dusting left-behind trophies, lingering over photographs.

I sit down at the piano and look at the sheets of music, scribbled on by different teachers for each child. I play a few notes and then stop to listen. Then silence fills the spaces. It's like an accordion closing in on itself, getting ready to open still wider.

Our oldest child is married. We have our first grandchild. They come to visit. I recently pulled down the carton of toys from the attic. My grandson rolls the red fire truck up and down the front hall. He builds tall towers with the old wooden blocks until they tumble down. The sounds condense on the windows.

In years to come will the echoes remain?

Grandson on Our Swing

A Three-Year-Old's Pace

OUR FIRST GRANDCHILD, ALMOST THREE, HAS COME from his home in France to stay with us. He takes my hand and holds it tight. I feel his small, warm fingers tugging mine and wonder where he will lead me.

His parents are on the other side of the ocean for two weeks. I hesitate to mention their names, not wanting to make him homesick. "You know, Grandmommy," he says at dinner time, "my mommy and daddy are all alone. They must miss me. Can we send them a card?"

I pull down the carton of games from upstairs in the attic. We play with the lottos and the dominos. Then I open the box of sewing cards and show him how to sew around the blue elephant. I hold the card and he sews. "Your father sewed this card when he was little," I tell him. "No," Paul says, "my father is big."

I find a nursery school for the mornings. The moment I hand him to the teacher, he throws himself on the floor and screams.

The teacher waves me away. When I return, he's playing with the other children.

The next day he says, "You know, Grandmommy, there's no school today." I tell him there's school each day during the week. When I take him back, he runs right off to play with his new friends. I stand at the school door empty-handed.

We go shopping. He sits contentedly in the shopping cart while I try to steer clear of the toys. Then we go look. I ask him to choose between a picture puzzle and a game of cards. "I want two toys," he says, "one, two." I shake my head. He repeats, "Two toys, Grandmommy. One, two." When I'm ready to give in, he chooses the picture puzzle and forgets the game of cards.

Upstairs, downstairs, fetch a toy, tie shoelaces, look for slippers, pick him up, put him down, pour him juice, fix his supper. I'm exhausted and, looking for a moment's rest, I sit down on the sofa. "Grandmommy, can we play another game?" he says. "Yes," I answer, "just one game, and then you can play by yourself." "No, Grandmommy, I can play with you."

I tell him that Granddaddy can play with him when he comes home from work. "Yes but Granddaddy comes home late, when it's dark." I tell him that it is not late, that it's suppertime when Granddaddy comes and that he will play with him after supper. "But you, too, Grandmommy. You can play with Granddaddy and me."

We buy a big bag of birdseed and fill the feeder in the cherry tree. Back inside, we wait for the birds to come. "Why don't they come when we're outside?" he asks. "Because they're afraid of us." He stands on the chair and looks out the window, watching them land on the little wooden platform and peck away at the grains. "But we won't hurt them," he says. "You go tell them, Grandmommy."

We take long walks down our road. He remembers each house, each front yard, each big oak tree, each mailbox, like a giant memory game. On the way back I sing him songs. I sing "If you're happy and you know it, clap your hands." He looks at me and claps his hands. "Again, Grandmommy!" I sing, the same verse over and over, and he claps his hands all the way home.

I peel and cut a yellow apple. "Do you want a piece?" At first he shakes his head. Then he waits close by until I ask him again. He takes a bite and asks for another piece. "You have good apples, Grandmommy," he says. I start to peel another apple. "Do you like Grandmommy's apples?" I want to hear him say it again and again.

At bath time, I collect lots of plastic cups and bowls, hoping to keep him quiet for a moment. I run the hot water the temperature he likes and pour in some bubble soap, just enough to play. Once he's in the tub, surrounded by toys and soapsuds, he says, "You stay here, Grandmommy. Don't go away." I kneel down by the side of the tub and he shows me a soap bubble. "Look, Grandmommy," he says, "there's a rainbow in it."

He has a small red plastic cassette player that he listens to as he goes to sleep. When it plays itself out, I return on tiptoe to try to make it play again. I put it in the wrong way. "No, Grandmommy," he says, opening his eyes, "that's not the way." And with deft little fingers, he takes out the cassette, turns it around the right way, and puts it back in. The next night he shows me again.

During the day, I hurry him along. If we're going outside, I hurry him into his jacket. If we're getting into the car, I hurry him onto his seat. If we're going to the store, I hurry him into the carriage. And then when we're finished shopping and we have to wait in a long line at the check-out counter, he leans his soft cheek against my hand and rubs it back and forth.

On Saturday, Pierre makes him pancakes. He learned from my father and uses the same recipe. Paul stands on a stool and watches. Then he asks if he can stir. He's not too happy stirring in the eggs, but once they disappeared into the batter, he's happy again. When the first pancakes are ready, he quickly moves to the table and waits to be served. I tell him I used to count my age in the number of pancakes I ate. He counts his twice, each time with maple syrup.

When we go to church, he stands up on my chair to watch. When he tires of standing, he sits on my lap. He doesn't talk or ask questions or move around. He just sits still and watches. I think back to when I took our children to church. Did they sit still and watch, or did I maybe try to explain too much?

We have an old swing in the front yard. I lower the ropes so Paul can sit on it alone. "Push me, Grandmommy," he says. I push him. "Push me higher, please, Grandmommy, push me higher!" He laughs and squirms when my hands catch him from the back, ready to push him higher. He doesn't turn around, he knows I'm there.

When the swing slows down, his blond hair glows in the sunlight, a spot of gold in the middle of the yard. I wait to see what he will do next. He gets up and steadies the wooden seat, then reaches around for my hand.

"Your turn, Grandmommy," he says. "I'll push you."

The American Grandmother

MOM DIDN'T WANT TO COME. EVER SINCE DAD DIED, FIVE years earlier, she wanted to stay put. "No more visits to Europe," she said. But there was to be a wedding. Our second child was getting married, and the presence of the American grandmother was requested.

We met her at the Geneva airport. All the children were waiting at the house. The tent was in place in the front yard for the wedding reception on Saturday. It was just family that evening. Mom asked to return to Dad's favorite restaurant on the lakeside.

Even the table was the same as the last time, the long table right next to the water. Mom looked out over the lake, up to the mountains, then back to each one of her grandchildren. We ordered fresh perch, Dad's choice.

Geneva in a Sea of Fog

Wild Daffodils

IT WAS AN EARLY SPRING AFTERNOON. PIERRE AND I were walking along a cross-country ski trail in the nearby Jura Mountains, no longer covered with snow. Clusters of wild daffodils, little yellow ones, dotted the dark green meadows. Geneva lay below, immersed in a white sea of fog. Beyond rose the Alps.

We had talked about Pierre's work and his plans—his career, his traveling around Europe, his frequent trips to the States. We had talked about the children—their work, their studies, their plans for the future. We were thinking about what each one of them was doing.

It was then that Pierre turned and asked me about my plans. I slowed my steps and searched for an answer. My mind went blank. I was in my fifties, and I had no plans for the future. I felt dizzy and sat down on the low stone wall that bordered the trail. I needed time. Pierre sat down alongside of me and waited.

Finding no answer, I said, "Why are you asking me that?"

"You are always asking me," he replied. "It's your turn. What do you want to do?"

As I sat there on the side of the mountain, with little daffodils pushing their way through the dark ground to the light, I realized I didn't have an answer. I didn't know what I wanted to do. Had I run out of script? I tried to catch my breath

Who was I? A wife, yes, a loving wife, for almost thirty years. A mother, yes, a loving mother, always listening or trying to listen. A daughter, still a daughter. A sister also. And a friend. Yet these roles were all in relationship to others—my husband, my children, my parents, my sister, my friends. Who was I all alone? Without these other people.

Who was I in relationship to myself?

I remembered the guessing game of my childhood—the tinker, tailor, soldier, sailor, and all the things I wanted to be. My world was then as wide as the whole blue sky under which I dreamed. What did I want to be back then? It wasn't anything like daughter, mother, husband-keeper. Nor did it rhyme with tinker, tailor, soldier, sailor, the words in the game. I wanted to be a violin player, maybe a soloist at Carnegie Hall, or I wanted to be a writer, maybe a poet like Edna St. Vincent Millay. I wanted to lie down in the grass, as she did in her poem "Renaissance," and look up until I could feel the sky come down upon me, "and—lo!—Infinity came down and settled over me. "

As a child, I spent long moments alone, reading and dreaming. I wrote down stories, short poems. And I practiced the violin. I played at recitals and in the conservatory orchestra. I wasn't a budding Edna St. Vincent Millay, nor was I a budding violin soloist. I was young, with time for still other dreams, so off I went to France—to fall in love with a French student.

We were the same age, at the same school, but we were as different as day and night. Back and forth we went over the ocean trying to make up our minds. When we were apart, our differences separated us still more. When we were together, the very same differences attracted us. Finally we chose to love one another and to stay together. We wanted our love to grow and blossom toward the sky.

At our wedding—in the church in Pocantico Hills, with both his parents and my parents present—we promised to each other that we would make it happen, that our love would blossom. I listened to the Old Testament reading about the worthy woman, whose husband is known at the city gates where he sits among the elders of the land. The reading begins, "A good wife, who can find her? She is far more precious than jewels..." I wanted to be the good wife. "She's always busy with wool and with flax; she does her work with willing hands..." (Proverbs 31, 1o–31) And I wanted to do my work with willing hands.

So while my husband sat at the city gates, I shopped and cooked and sewed and washed. I took care of my household. My hands were never idle. I looked after the children, tending their tempers. I looked after my husband, following him around Europe. And I took my place wherever I could.

No more the tinker, tailor, no longer the violin player, or the poet. I was wife, mother, and housekeeper. The years went by, gathering momentum, like a ball of yarn, unrolling, always faster. The older children became adolescents, the younger children became older. There were always more hands to hold, more errands to do, more meals to prepare. I continued to look well to the ways of my household. The older children went off to university. I remained busy with the younger ones. There was now more time for them. Soon they, too, left home.

And then, what does the worthy woman do? When her household is all taken care of? When the nights grow quiet and the days grow long? When her children go off and the house is empty? What then does the worthy woman do?

Once, many years earlier, in between shopping and taking care of the house, I stopped for a moment and went home with a friend to her house. We'd been busy with errands all morning. We were both tired and worn out. She still had a young child who'd been fussing in the stroller most of the morning. My friend put her child in the playpen and excused herself to go take a shower. She said she wanted "to refresh herself." I sat stunned and speechless in her kitchen. She had put her young child and her friend aside in order to refresh herself. And in the middle of the day.

The incident must have stayed in the back of my mind because when Pierre asked me that afternoon up in the Jura Mountains what I wanted to do and when I finally found an answer, I said I wanted to refresh myself. And I said that once I was refreshed—I wanted to write, to write about how it felt to take time for myself.

I would write in old-fashioned notebooks, not on the bits and pieces of paper as in years past—love notes to my husband, remembrances to each child, letters to family and friends, thoughts jotted down in the margins of books. All my scattered scribblings, I'd stitch them together into stories. I would write about falling in love with a Frenchman, about raising children and moving from country to country, about the water jug and its crack. About the wild daffodils that come up each spring in the Jura Mountains, the ones that were poking their heads through the dark earth all around us.

Today we live alone in our house, and I write. The smallest bedroom, the one that once was our youngest son's, that rang with his nightmares month after month, has become my writing place. I sit at my old oak desk, the drawers now filled with stories. I push back the white curtain and look out my window over the front yard, the swings, the old cherry tree, beyond the high hedges.

I close my eyes and look within.

My Window, Geneva

Recipe Index

Credits

Earlier versions of these stories (very often with different titles) have appeared in the following periodicals and anthologies.

Swaying, *The Christian Science Monitor*, Boston, 08/91; *Swaying*, University of Iowa Press, 1996

Footsteps, *The Messenger*, Padua, Italy, 1989

Spécialité Provençale, *Albany Review*, Albany, 05/88; *Two Worlds Walking*, New Rivers Press, 1994

Lace Curtains, *The Christian Science Monitor*, Boston, 05/90

Birthdays, *The Courier*, Geneva, 9/89

Remember, *The Courier*, Geneva, 11/99

Aggiornamento, *Resident Abroad, London Financial Times*, London, 11/86

Quarantine Regulations, *Resident Abroad, London Financial Times*, London, 04/87

Il Nonno, *Offshoots III, Writing from Geneva*, Geneva, 1995

Black and White, *Offshoots IV, Writing from Geneva*, Geneva, 1997

Emilia's Petition, *Resident Abroad, London Financial Times*, London, 08/86

Swiss Scaffolding, *Resident Abroad, London Financial Times*, London, 09/86

I'm Here, *Resident Abroad, London Financial Times*, London, 10/86

The Straw Chair, *The Christian Science Monitor*, Boston, 09/88; Home
    Forum Reader, Boston, 1990

His Story, Our Story, *The Christian Science Monitor*, Boston, 12/88

Once a Year, *The Christian Science Monitor*, 09/93

The Water Jug, *The Messenger,* Padua, Italy, 1986

La Bête Noire, *Resident Abroad, London Financial Times*, London, 01/87

Red Geraniums, *The Country*, Pine Plains, NY, 09/98; *Tanzania on Tuesday*,
    New Rivers Press, 1997

The Old House, *The Country,* Pine Plains, NY, 01/98

Graffiti at the Lycée, *France Today*, San Francisco, 10/86

In the Light, *Offshoots IV, Writing from Geneva*, Geneva, 1997

Ode to the Potato, *The Christian Science Monitor*, 05/89;

Cupid's Wild Arrows, Bergli Books, Basel, 91

The Chesterfields of Grandmère, *The Country*, Pine Plains, NY, 07/98

Flashbacks, *The Reality of Breastfeeding, Reflections by Contemporary Women*,
    editors A. B. Brown, K. R. McPherson, 1998

Echoes, *The Christian Science Monitor*, Boston, 11/96;

Ticking Along Too, Bergli Books, Basel, 96

A Three-Year-Old's Pace, *The Christian Science Monitor*, Boston, 02/95

Wild Daffodils, T*he Christian Science Monitor*, Boston, 05/95

PHOTOGRAPHS

Cover: Scala Santa Maria del Monte, Italy; Davide Ragusa

Page 6: Grenoble, 1955; *Cap*, Photo Press, Grenoble

Page 15: Cloister, Pavia; Susan Marquardt

Page 15: Gardens, Lago di Como; Pierre-Yves Tiberghien

Page 16: Snow-Covered Trail in Haute Savoie; Susan Tiberghien

Page 24: Countryside, Provence; Karen L. McDermott

Page 38: La Grande Place, Brussels; Pierre-Yves Tiberghien

Page 56: Church, Northern Italy; Karen L. McDermott

Page 62: Our Balcony, Comerio; Susan Tiberghien

Page 68: Countryside near Lago Maggiore; Karen L. McDermott

Page 88: Le Lac de Genève; Karen L. McDermott

Page 96: Our Apartment Building, Geneva; Susan Tiberghien

Page 104: The Straw Chair, Saigon; Phu My Orphanage, Saigon

Page 112: Welcoming Daniel; Susan Tiberghien

Page 122: The Water Jug, Geneva; Susan Tiberghien

Page 132: Samoëns in Winter; Photo Editions, Combier- Mâcon

Page 140: The Hay Chalet; Pierre-Yves Tiberghien

Page 153: Red Geraniums, Samoëns; Susan Tiberghien

Page 156: The Old House, Prévessin; Pierre-Yves Tiberghien

Page 166: The Statue of Voltaire, Ferney; Susan Tiberghien

Page 178: 90th Birthday, Tourcoing; Pierre-Yves Tiberghien

Page 192: Our House, Geneva; Susan Tiberghien

Page 202: Our Front Door; Susan Tiberghien

Page 210: Grandson on Our Swing, Geneva; Susan Tiberghien

Page 218: Geneva in a Sea of Fog; Pierre-Yves Tiberghien

Page 224: My Window, Geneva; Susan Tiberghien

Susan M. Tiberghien

230

About the Author

SUSAN TIBERGHIEN IS THE AUTHOR OF THREE MEMOIRS and the bestselling nonfiction book, *One Year to a Writing Life*. Her first book, *Looking for Gold: A Year in Jungian Analysis*, was published when she turned sixty.

Her most recent title, *Side by Side: Writing Your Love Story*, shares her love for a Frenchman and her love for writing. *Footsteps: In Love with a Frenchman* is the behind the scenes chronicle of Tiberghien's emerging writer's life.

Tiberghien has taught creative writing for over twenty-five years at writers' centers and conferences across the States and Europe, at C. G. Jung Societies, for the International Women's Writing Guild, and each month for the Geneva Writers' Group that she founded twenty years ago. She lives in Geneva with her French husband. Some of her six children live close by, the others live in Paris and in Brooklyn.